Tithe and Offering
Where Pastors Err

BY

AKHADIN PRUDENCE

Tate Publishing, LLC

Dedication

To the Church of God all over the world

Acknowledgements

At a time, I was not sure I wanted to continue to write this book but many people encouraged me through the process. Now that it is completed, I want to acknowledge everyone who contributed to the success of the work.

I thank God - who is Head over all - for the grace to start and finish this work.

Thank you Charles Dyquo, Mike Atoh, for your encouragements, creative ideas, and criticism of my thoughts in the book. You are a pillar of strength.

To my colleagues, a heart felt thank you for your tremendous support and encouragement.

To my siblings, I admire your faith in my work.

Thanks to the Church of God, you are my inspiration.

Table of Contents

Foreword

Authors are like preachers: they all have messages to communicate. The concern of the author is the total neglect of the poor and needy in most of our churches, and if possible, the total eradication of the excesses of some pastors who manipulate the word of God to suit their reasons for getting money from the people through tithe and various shades of offering.

The author is not against the payment of the tithe and offering, but argues that if the Pastors require them from God's people, then the Pastors are bound to disburse tithes and offering according to scripture.

To strengthen her argument, she went on to research on the Biblical view of the subject. Consequently, the reader will find the book studded with many Bible passages.

Added to the issue of the neglect of the poor, the book speaks against many teachings intended to persuade the congregation into giving. The book criticizes the doctrines of sowing into the anointing, sowing to break yokes, tithing to participate in the breaking of bread; borrowing to sow a seed for prosperity is criticized using the scriptures

Her strong belief is that no offering is forced, and that the best way to lay up treasures in heaven is to give to the poor. The book is of the view that any church will grow if only pastors and church leaders realize and pay proper attention to the needs of the poor in the church.

I pray that pastors who earnestly desire a numerical growth for their congregations will read this book and make appropriate adjustments. They will soon realize that what they spend millions to achieve through advertisements can easily be gotten through charity and love toward their flocks.

Atoh A. Aigbomian

Preface

The best things in life are freely given. Love, sunshine, rain, life, health, air, and peace are freely given by God to man. Jesus Christ, the Savior of the world was also freely given. The best therefore, that could be said to have been given by man to God are things freely and willingly given. God is not a God of force and does not apply the rule of force. Love is the basis of God's dealing with man for man's benefit.

It is expected also that the principles of love and freedom should apply in our giving, whether of praises, worship, thanksgiving, tithe, and offering to God. This is why the force with which church leaders preach the message of tithe and offering has become a subject for discussion.

This book, "Tithe and Offering - Where Pastors Err," looks at the genesis of this tradition as explained in theology in the light of other traditions like the Sabbath, Circumcision, and Burnt Offerings. The author takes a journey to the wilderness, where God gave commandments concerning tithes and offerings. When God called for tithe and offering from His people, it was for all in God's House - the Priests, the Levites and the People were all partakers of the meat in God's House. The call for tithe and offerings in the New Testament Church is criticized in the light of God's Word concerning the ordinances in the Old Testament Church. While the message of bringing in tithes and offerings into God's house is zealously preached in churches, no one seems to know anything about making this meat available to God's people. Talking about making meat available for God's people is considered impossible, not relevant, or just a taboo. According to some teachings, it is meat for a class of people or just meant for the maintenance of God's house alone or doing God's business.

This book examines giving in the early Church revealing that the giving to God in the New Testament was to the Saints of God and to good work in the house of God.

This book calls on Pastors to read the scriptures again with a good and honest heart and take away the yoke of fear and the curse of the devourer that has been knowingly or unknowingly introduced into the lives of God's people by the hard and forceful teaching on tithes and offerings.

Introduction

One day I watched a drama on a television station. In the drama, a man sought the help of a prophet who claimed to possess power to foretell the future. The prophet promised the man protection in "the name of the Lord" and admonished him to dedicate his life to God. Part of the dedication to God included the giving of all he had. In fear and obedience to this instruction, the man, who was also an average income earner, gave some money to the church. The man later lost his job and was paid all entitlement. He informed the prophet of this development, but received the divine instruction to give/sow all the entitlement as seed for a greater business.

Though puzzled, the man went ahead to issue a check to the church. The prophet gratefully received the check and did something else that baffled me: As he put the check away and the man was about to leave, the prophet, with a gruesome smile on his face said, "Brother, the church needs a television. The Lord bless you as you get one for the church."

Though perplexed, he gave the only television set in his house to the church, since he had no money to buy another one. Could not the church have used part of the money already received to acquire the television set required? I pondered within. I actually thought the drama was over- exaggerated and that no church or pastor would do such a thing. However, I was wrong.

I have listened to renowned preachers preach on this subject in churches, television and radio stations. I have also read books written by different Bible teachers. I have watched in astonishment the passion with which the message of giving tithes and offerings is delivered and adminis-

tered in some churches. Since the Word of God is accessible to everyone, I decided to do a study on this wonderful topic to find the Bible's teaching on the issue.

I share in this book astounding knowledge from the study and trust that it would be a source of blessing to the Church, for no matter what has been preached, God's Word remains the authority on issues that relate to the doctrine of the Church.

"All scripture is given by inspiration of God, and is profitable for doctrine, for reproof, for correction, for instruction in righteousness: That the man of God may be perfect, thoroughly furnished unto all good works." (2 Timothy 3:16–17)

The Bible admonishes the Christian to study and be an approved laborer who accurately handles and communicates the word of truth (1 Timothy 2:15). The call to divide rightly or interpret God's Word means there is the possibility to interpret it wrongly. The Word of God is only fruitful in a good and honest heart; only such a heart can truly and rightly understand and communicate God's Word.

Chapter One

THE DOCTRINE OF TITHE AND OFFERING

Some Christians argue that the doctrine of Tithing came with the Law of Moses, and is therefore, not binding on the Church like every other Law of Moses. Rather it has been fulfilled and abolished by the reason of the sacrifice of Jesus Christ on the cross. Some other Christians argue that tithing has its roots from Abraham who gave a tithe of all he had to Melchizedek the priest of God. These say that Christians who claim right to the blessings of Abraham ought to give tithes (give a tenth part of all increases) as he gave. Whatever way anyone may have analyzed the issue of tithing, the Bible holds the ultimate truth.

We live in times when people do or say anything to make money. Many finance conventions are being organized. Messages and teachings on different forms of giving are preached. So much emphasis is placed on giving to God. Some preach that the power of life and death, and the key to prosperity lies in how much one can give.

I have seen a sick man instructed to sow seeds (give money) for his healing. I have seen the needy instructed to give the last of what they have so that God can bless them with what they do not have. I have seen cases where money is collected from the needy, the hungry, the homeless and the widow to give to the rich in the name of tapping into the anointing some man possesses. I have watched pastors grow fatter and live in affluence while the congregations shamefully live in lack.

The blessing of prosperity has been arrogated to

one's ability to give to God and if one is needy and do lack, it is interpreted to mean that such people do not give. I have heard testimonies of how God would not answer prayers until some money was sowed to Him as seed so much that I wonder whether God by chance may have turned His attention from the sacrifice of Jesus Christ to the sacrifices of man.

Something must be wrong!

THE MISUSE

There are churches where believers have to give on a daily basis and for every small project the church embarks on, even to the smallest project of buying a pastor's lunch. The moneys given as tithes and offerings which includes seed offerings, thanksgiving offerings, special offerings, building offerings, programme offerings, love offerings, help offerings, etc. are stashed away in accounts in some banks. They are only signed away to the "headquarters" or when an eminent member of the church is marrying or has an occasion to celebrate. Well, this is exactly the case in a church where I once worshiped. In fact, the inspiration to carry out this study emanated from watching what happened daily in this church. I watched as brethren gave, not because of the conviction from God's Word but because of the embarrassments of been seen not to be responsive to the call to give. After each meeting, you find these brethren begging money from other brethren because they gave all they had. Some seemingly smart brethren, to avoid embarrassment simply just make pledges they do not intend to redeem saying they made it in faith.

If a member loses mother or father, he is on his own, if a woman loses a husband, brethren are there to pay condolence visits and after that, the family is abandoned or advised to sow to God in order to survive. Participating in the burial of a member's loved one is not in the question, much more so as Jesus Christ had said, "let the dead bury the dead," let alone giving to the bereaved in such circumstance.

Yet, the church calls out in every service for tithes, offerings, and pledges. It is either a pledge for a programme, or pledges to fund one pastor's housing, transport, birthday, or marriage. The church is taxed even when relatives of church leaders who may not be members are marking special days. Sometimes when they cared to speak the word of knowledge concerning giving to the brethren's need, the money never gets to those in whose stead the word of giving came. It is stashed away in an account where only the leaders can draw at their convenience.

Every meeting is a meeting to give because believers are not supposed to come empty-handed into God's house. Brethren who have nothing to give stay away at home to avoid embarrassment. Pledges are made to rent or build places of worship; pledges are made to redecorate the church or change furniture even when there is no need to do so. To these pastors, being able to announce that something (whether useful or useless to the member) has been bought is just another activity in church. To them, it is achievement to announce how much they have raised and how rich the church has become. But not one call is made to provide room for the homeless in the same church; not one pledge to aid widows, orphans, and the fatherless in the church; not one pledge for brethren who cannot afford school fees, or for families who cannot put food on their table.

The unemployed in the congregation are told to borrow and give. The brethren that have are encouraged to give all to God, to sow into God and into the anointing of a group leader or pastor. What we see at work is the same spirit of greed, covetousness, and selfish ambition, which is typical of the world's government where leaders take advantage of

the people. The church now has a leadership that does not care for the people, but pile up as many riches as they can to satisfy their lust for wealth, power and fame. They rule over the flock of God as if God has handed the power of the lives of His people to them.

It is really amazing watching and listening as Christian leaders interpret God's messages always in their own favor. The pastors are quick to preach from Malachi 3:10, "Bring ye all the tithes into my storehouse," but pretend that the next phrase " . . . that there may be meat in mine house," does not exist. They do not allude to verses in the Bible that say what the tithe is used for or who should eat the meat in God's house. According to them, tithes and offerings are hallowed and belong to God; so no questions should be asked about how it is spent. They are quick to preach that a woman gave of her last morsel to Elijah but fail to point out that Elijah did not ask the woman until he was instructed of God. They are quick to preach about how two men on hearing David wish for the water of Bethlehem risked their lives to get him water from the well and pretend that the story ended there. They never mention that the same Bible recorded that David would not drink the water, but poured it unto God; because according to him, he was not worthy of the lives of the men, who had risked their lives to get him water. They just keeping preaching on giving and it does not matter whether the giver has to steal to afford it.

Tithes and offerings, where did it all start? Is it part of the new will? What does Jesus Christ say about them? How do they apply to the Church today?

TITHE

The word "tithe" was first introduced in Genesis 14:18–20 in an encounter between two great personalities: Melchizedek the Priest of the Most High God and Abraham the friend of the Most High God.

And Melchizedek king of Salem brought forth bread and wine: and he was the priest of the most high God. And he blessed him, and said, Blessed be Abram of the most high God, possessor of heaven and earth: And blessed be the most high God, which hath delivered thine enemies into thy hand. And he gave him tithes of all.
(Genesis 14:18–20)

It is preached that Father Abraham first gave tithe long before the Law of Moses. Reading the chapters before Genesis 14, there is no record that God ever spoke to Abraham or any one before him on tithing or giving. Melchizedek cannot be said to have demanded it either. In fact, there is nothing in the whole passage (Genesis 14:1–24) that suggests that Abraham gave tithe. On the contrary, the pointer is to the Priest Melchizedek who went to meet him on his return from the mission to rescue his nephew. Let us consider the phrases in the passage:

And Melchizedek king of Salem brought forth bread and wine
And he was the priest of the most high God
And he blessed him and said, Blessed be Abram
of the most high God . . .
And he gave him tithes of all.

It is possible and does make sense to think Abraham gave tithe to the priest of God because one is a priest and the other a man who has returned from battle with some goods. Yet, in the meeting of the two personalities - the priest of the Most High God and Abraham of the Most High God, Genesis 14:18–20 clearly states that one of the personalities brought something. It is not Abraham, but the priest Melchizedek who came with bread and wine. Has anyone bothered pondering the purpose of the bread and wine?

The phrases above could be said to refer to one and same person considering the use of the pronoun "he" and the conjunction "and." "Melchizedek king of Salem brought forth bread and wine, and he was the priest of the most high God, and he blessed Abraham . . . And he gave him tithe of all." The "he" in the passage points to Melchizedek.

The Priest of the Most High God brought bread and wine, blessed Abraham and gave him tithe of bread and wine. This can be inferred for many reasons: First, the goods referred to in Chapter Fourteen of Genesis did not belong to Abraham. It is important to note that throughout the chapter, the Bible used the term "goods" and not "spoil." The goods belonged to the people of Sodom and Gomorrah who were carried away during the war. Lot, Abraham's nephew was among the captives. Abraham had pursued the captors, rescued and brought back all the people and their goods (not spoils) that were carried away. How could Abraham have given tithe of goods that were not his? Even when the King of Sodom offered him the goods, Abraham answered,

. . . I have lift up mine hand unto the LORD, the most high God, the possessor of heaven and earth, that I will not take from a thread even to a shoe latchet, and that I will not take any thing that is thine, lest thou shouldest say, I have made Abram rich: Save only that which the young men have eaten,

and the portion of the men which went with me, Aner, Eshcol,
and Mamre; let them take their portion.
(Genesis 14:22–24)

What Abraham took from the goods was that which his young men had eaten and the share for the men who went on the rescue mission with him. He did not say anything about paying tithe out of the goods to Melchizedek unless he could be said to have told a half-truth. Furthermore, it never entered the heart of Abraham to consider the goods his, for he said to the king of Sodom "I will not take anything that is thine." He was met by Melchizedek at the Valley of Shaveh, the king's dale, a place that was not his home, far away from what was his to give away as tithe. How then could Abraham have given the priest tithe of goods he considered not honorable enough for him to accept? Why would he give something he had no respect for to the Possessor of heaven and earth?

Paul, in Hebrews 7:12–17 likened the priesthood of Jesus Christ to that of Melchizedek and compared it with the priesthood of Aaron. Apart from the analogy made by Paul, we can draw some more from the meeting between Melchizedek and Abraham, and show that in all spiritual consideration that the priest gave a tithe and not Abraham.

In the priesthood of Aaron, the people of Israel went to the priest with an offering. However, to signify that God was going to come to man with an offering, Melchizedek met Abraham instead, blessed him and offered him bread and wine, an action that would have typified the giving of the body and the blood of Jesus Christ for mankind.

With Abraham, God provided Himself a lamb for the burnt offering, bread and wine for the tithe. In the priesthood, in the order of Melchizedek, Jesus Christ the High Priest came to man bearing with him the items required for sacrifice–His body and blood. He offered them up for man's salvation. This is quite different for the priesthood of Aaron, where the people carry to the priest tithes, burnt offerings, and sacrifices.

Even if it is true from interpretation that Abraham gave tithe, there is no record that God required or commanded it. Melchizedek also did not request it. The only logical reason (if we must apply logics to God's Word) is that Abraham gave of his own freewill in love and faith according to his revelation of God. It was not forced or commanded. God's promises to Abraham were not hinged on the giving of tithe to Melchizedek or on any good work at that, but on faith in God. God decided to bless a man; He searched out Abraham and told him of His intention. Abraham believed God and his believing was credited to him as righteousness (Genesis 15:6).

Yet, the church views this meeting differently and has decided that this is enough reason to hold the new creation to this ordinance. When one asks the reason that a Christian should tithe, it is easy to say, "Abraham did it. If we must lay claims to the blessings of Abraham, we must follow his example." If we follow this line of theology, then there is another ordinance that existed before the Law and greater than tithing - the Sabbath.

The ordinances of the Sabbath existed from creation when God rested after six days of work.

And on the seventh day God ended his work which he had made; and he rested on the seventh day from all his work which he had made. And God blessed the seventh day, and sanctified it: because that in it he had rested from all his work which God created and made. (Genesis 2:2–3)

The Sabbath - the ordinance of rest - dates back to creation. The Bible says God ended and rested from work on the seventh day after working six days. He therefore sanctified the seventh day as a day of rest. This is one ordinance whose origin was God Himself. Tithing was between Melchizedek and Abraham, but God who is greater than all observed the Sabbath. He rested and therefore called upon all of His creation to rest from work on the seventh day of every week.

God continued to stress the seriousness of this ordinance in his dealing with the children of Israel in the wilderness and through the prophets. The ordinance was to be observed throughout all generations. Servants were to go free after seven years (Exodus 21:2); lands were to be left fallow after seven years (Exodus 23:11).

Six days thou shalt do thy work, and on the seventh day thou shalt rest: that thine ox and thine ass may rest, and the son of thy handmaid, and the stranger, may be refreshed. (Exodus 23:12)

It was to be a sign between Him and His people forever; the consequence of disobeying it was death.

Six days may work be done; but in the seventh is the Sabbath of rest, holy to the LORD: whosoever doeth any work in the Sabbath day, he shall surely be put to death. Wherefore the children of Israel shall keep the Sabbath, to observe the Sabbath throughout their generations, for a perpetual covenant. It is a sign between me and the children of Israel for ever: for in six days the LORD made heaven and earth, and on the seventh day he rested, and was refreshed. (Exodus 31:15–17)

But the seventh day is the Sabbath of the LORD thy God: in it thou shalt not do any work, thou, nor thy son, nor thy daughter, thy manservant, nor thy maidservant, nor thy cattle, nor thy stranger that is within thy gates: For in six days the

LORD made heaven and earth, the sea, and all that in them is, and rested the seventh day: wherefore the LORD blessed the Sabbath day, and hallowed it. (Exodus 20:10–11)

Isaiah prophesying concerning the last days, confirmed the Sabbath an everlasting covenant: An ordinance that would continue forever in the new heaven and earth, and will be binding on all nations of the earth.

For as the new heavens and the new earth, which I will make, shall remain before me, saith the LORD, so shall your seed and your name remain. And it shall come to pass, that from one new moon to another, and from one sabbath to another, shall all flesh come to worship before me, saith the LORD. (Isaiah 66:22–23).

Even Jesus Christ - the mediator of the New Testament - when He walked the earth observed the Sabbath (Luke 4:16). Yet, some churches consider this ordinance of the Sabbath void because of the sacrifice of the Son of God on the cross. They choose to go to church on Sunday instead of Saturday. They even scoff at Christians who still observe the Sabbath even though in the end, both the tithe payer and the Sabbath worshiper end up the same, being debtors to the Law.

Another ordinance that started from days of conscience into the Law and Prophet was the law of Burnt Offering:

And Noah builded an altar unto the LORD; and took of every clean beast, and of every clean fowl, and offered burnt offerings on the altar. And the LORD smelled a sweet savour; and the LORD said in his heart, I will not again curse the ground any more. (Genesis 8: 20–21)

The ordinance, which was also of freewill started from the time of Abel, who brought the sacrifice of the "first-ling of his flock and the fat thereof" (Genesis 4:4). It continued through the world that started with Noah, long before the encounter between the priest Melchizedek and Abraham, through the Law and the Prophets. The daily life of anyone who had walked with God before the coming of Jesus Christ was not complete without a burnt offering onto God. These days, no one is seen offering up sheep and goats as sacrifice unto God, the Father of the Lord Jesus Christ because of faith in the perfect sacrifice of His Son on the cross.

Abraham in his walk with God also offered sacrifices of rams, goat, hcifer, turtledove, pigeon, and even his son when God requested Isaac of him. If Abraham gave tithe, he gave it to one who was a king and priest, but to God he gave burnt offerings because God required it of him.

Therefore, if pastors think it scriptural for the New Testament Church to tithe because Abraham did the same, then it would also be right to start carrying out burnt offerings in the church. Truth, they say, is parallel! God's instruction to Abraham to offer sacrifices of rams, goat, heifer, turtledove and pigeon should be a more tenable reason to carry on with the ordinance of burnt offerings. The Church then should offer burnt offerings to God much more that God swore to the covenant of giving the Promised Land after the sacrifice.

The ordinance of burnt offering attracted blessings and promises from God: He gave the promise of the rain bow as a check on His anger against the sins of the world after Noah's burnt offering to Him. The Church should really be zealous therefore to carry on with it. But this is not so because the Church has been able to accept and believe that the sacrifice of Jesus Christ on the cross has abolished the ordinances of burning sacrifices to God. It is considered idolatry in the today's world to see anyone burn anything as part of worship to God.

The covenant of circumcision is another very significant ordinance in God's dealing with Abraham.

And God said unto Abraham, Thou shalt keep my covenant therefore, thou, and thy seed after thee in their generations. This is my covenant, which ye shall keep, between me and you and thy seed after thee; Every man child among you shall be circumcised. And ye shall circumcise the flesh of your foreskin; and it shall be a token of the covenant betwixt me and you. And he that is eight days old shall be circumcised among you, every man child in your generations, he that is born in the house, or bought with money of any stranger, which is not of thy seed. He that is born in thy house, and he that is bought with thy money, must needs be circumcised: and my covenant shall be in your flesh for an everlasting covenant. And the uncircumcised man child whose flesh of his foreskin is not circumcised, that soul shall be cut off from his people; he hath broken my covenant. (Genesis 17:9–14)

Just like the promise, the covenant of circumcision was to Abraham and his seed. Jesus Christ as the seed of Abraham was circumcised. If the Church is so interested in following the foot-steps of Abraham, I wonder why we have not heard any teaching yet on bringing all male children to God's house for circumcision on the eighth day, the Church being Abraham's seed. Abraham was not instructed to give tithe, but was commanded in God's own words to keep the covenant of circumcision.

Thou shalt keep my covenant therefore, thou, and thy seed after thee in their generations. This is my covenant, which ye shall keep, between me and you and thy seed after thee.

The Church should also start the ceremony of circumcision and start to lay much emphasis on it as it is doing with tithes and offerings or face the danger of being cut off. That a priest circumcised Jesus in the synagogue should also be a tenable reason to ask Christians to bring their male children to church to be circumcised. But nobody is preaching this message. One therefore, wonders why the Church still exists as the Body of Christ to this moment, since it is not keeping so fearful a covenant that carries such great consequences—the soul of the offender being cut off from God's people. This is not so because the church has been able to accept the grace to be free from the ordinance by the reason of the sacrifice of Jesus Christ.

If the Church therefore considered that the sacrifice of Jesus Christ on the cross has made these everlasting laws of the Sabbath, burnt offering and circumcision void, what is special about tithing and offerings that the blood did not handle? Yet some church leaders have preached that God could put yokes on the lives of Christians for not tithing and sometimes attribute calamities in a Christian's life to nonpayment of tithes and offering! Talk of the cankerworm and caterpillar that they say God or the devil sends to devour God's children when they do not pay their tithe. It is preached that yokes would not be broken until an offering of money is given at the altar and that a Christian has no business taking part in the communion except that he or she is a tithe payer.

These teachings are strange and have no scriptural backbone. By the teaching, pastors infer that the offering of some currency notes probably printed by some unbelieving group of people is stronger than, or may be, complement the sacrifice of the blood of the Lamb of God. They infer that there is a power in money that can break yokes that faith in the name and the blood of Jesus Christ cannot break. To teach that there are yokes that cannot be broken until Christians put money on the altar is crucifying the Son of God afresh. They infer that the offering of Jesus on the cross was not perfect or complete. But if striking the Rock the second time when he was told to speak to it were unforgivable and beyond pardon for Moses, then will it be unpardonable for anyone to teach that a Christian must offer money to God to be utterly free from bondage or to receive blessings already freely given by God in Christ Jesus.

The Bible witnesses that Jesus Christ blotted out the handwriting of ordinances that were opposed and hostile to us, and took them out of the way, having nailed them to the cross (Colossians 2:14). One such written code that is nailed to the cross is the curse of the devourer. God has offered Jesus Christ and the sacrifice is finished, the offering is complete and perfect!

And you, being dead in your sins and the uncircumcision of your flesh, hath he quickened together with him, having forgiven you all trespasses; blotting out the handwriting of ordinances that was against us, which was contrary to us, and took it out of the way, nailing it to his cross; And having spoiled principalities and powers, he made a show of them openly, triumphing over them in it. Let no man therefore judge you in meat, or in drink, or in respect of an holyday, or of the new moon, or of the Sabbath days: Which are a shadow of things to come; but the body is of Christ. Let no man beguile you of your reward in a voluntary humility and worshipping of angels, intruding into those things which he hath not seen, vainly puffed up by his fleshly mind, . . .
(Colossians 2:14–18)

Why then would God's shepherds bring the flock purchased by His own blood to judgment on tithes and offerings? Why would any man condemn any member of God's

Church for not sowing into the anointing? Why would a pastor wish calamity upon a member because he or she earns income that he could not bring to God?

Paul admonishing the church in his letter to Galatians wrote:

For I testify again to every man that is circumcised that he is a debtor to do the whole law. Christ is become of no effect unto you, whosoever of you are justified by the law; ye are fallen from grace." (Galatians 5:3–4)

The law of circumcision was given to Abraham. That could have been one reason the early church insisted that the Gentile Christians be circumcised. Paul spoke in defense of grace through Jesus Christ. The circumcision, though given to Abraham, was considered law to the New Testament Church. However, living by the law nullifies grace through Jesus—Christ is made of no effect. Living by the ordinance (circumcision) given to Abraham was falling from grace. Abraham lived, according to theology in the days of conscience, but the church live in the dispensation of grace. Grace has no relationship with conscience; grace is grace and not conscience.

A pastor therefore has no scriptural backing to hold or despise a Christian for not tithing. Tithing was not commanded in the days of Abraham. There was no blessing or causing to it either. But if they cannot let go this ordinance, then the shepherds of God should look again into God's Word and discover God's desire in the administration of His Church with respect to tithes and offering, if the Church must keep this law.

Chapter Two

TITHE AND OFFERING IN THE LAW

From the foundations of the earth, God desired a people. This dream came to pass in the children of Israel the seed of Abraham. He is the Father and therefore put in place a plan on how He wanted His house administered. He commanded Moses to build a sanctuary to represent His presence amongst his people. Of the twelve tribes of Israel, He took the tribe of Levi unto Himself, and Aaron and his sons as His priests for the work in the Sanctuary. He had to make provisions for everyone who was part of His house and for the tribe unto whom He had said, "You shall have no inheritance." He said in Malachi 3:10a, "Bring your tithes and offering that there may be meat in my house." To this intent, God instituted the ordinance of tithe and offering, He spoke with Moses about it for the first time since creation and gave directives on the giving and administering of tithe and offerings in the sanctuary. These included the tithes and offerings that were to God, tithes and offerings to the Levite and tithes and offerings to the people.

TITHES AND OFFERINGS TO GOD

A study of the books of the Law shows that there was giving that was holy onto the Lord. They belonged to God (Exodus 22:29–30, Numbers 3:11–13).

And the LORD spake unto Moses, saying, Sanctify unto me

all the firstborn, whatsoever openeth the womb among the children of Israel, both of man and of beast: it is mine. . . . That thou shalt set apart unto the LORD all that openeth the matrix, and every firstling that cometh of a beast which thou hast; the males shall be the LORD'S. And every firstling of an ass thou shalt redeem with a lamb; and if thou wilt not redeem it, then thou shalt break his neck: and all the firstborn of man among thy children shalt thou redeem. (Exodus 13:1, 12–13)

After the killing of the firstborn of man and beast in Egypt, and before the crossing of the Red Sea, God spoke to Moses on the dedication and separation of all firstborn in Israel. Israel was to separate their firstborn of man and beast, fruits and liquor to God. This was because He had to kill the firstborn of every Egyptian and their beasts to compel the Pharaoh of Egypt to let Israel leave the bondage in Egypt.

The giving of every firstborn of man, beast, fruits and liquor was not a kind of tithing. It was the giving of every first thing in the life of an Israelite because of the Passover in Egypt. It could be said to be the giving of the first place and the first of everything in our lives to God. In the place of every firstborn that opens the womb in Israel, God took to Himself the tribe of Levi.

And the LORD spake unto Moses, saying, And I, behold, I have taken the Levites from among the children of Israel instead of all the firstborn that openeth the matrix among the children of Israel: therefore the Levites shall be mine; because all the firstborn are mine; for on the day that I smote all the firstborn in the land of Egypt I hallowed unto me all the firstborn in Israel, both man and beast: mine shall they be: I am the LORD. (Numbers 3:11–13)

All offerings of food and animals offered by fire

(Burnt Offerings) were the Lord's (Lev 1:6 - 17, 6:8–12).

"But he shall wash the inwards and the legs with water: and the priest shall bring it all, and burn it upon the altar: it is a burnt sacrifice, an offering made by fire, of a sweet savour unto the LORD." (Leviticus 1:13)

The tithes of land and the seeds and fruits thereof (seeds and fruits from the land given as tithe) belonged to God.

And all the tithe of the land, whether of the seed of the land, or of the fruit of the tree, is the LORD'S: it is holy unto the LORD. And if a man will at all redeem ought of his tithes, he shall add thereto the fifth part thereof. (Leviticus 27:30–31)

A tenth part of the tithe (A portion of tithe when divided into ten portions) of the flocks belonged to the Lord.

*And concerning the tithe of the herd, or of the flock, even of whatsoever passeth under the rod, the tenth shall be holy unto the LORD. He shall not search whether it be good or bad, neither shall he change it: and if he change it at all, then both it and the change thereof shall be holy; it shall not be redeemed.
(Leviticus 27:32–33)*

TITHES AND OFFERINGS TO WORKERS OF THE SANCTUARY

There were tithes that belonged to the workers of the sanctuary - The Levites. These parts were given to the Levites because they did not own properties. They were to dedicate their lives completely to the services of the Sanctuary. God was their inheritance!

And, behold, I have given the children of Levi all the tenth in Israel for an inheritance, for their service which they serve, even the service of the tabernacle of the congregation. (Numbers 18:21)

But the tithes of the children of Israel, which they offer as an heave offering unto the LORD, I have given to the Levites to inherit: therefore I have said unto them, Among the children of Israel they shall have no inheritance. (Numbers 18:24)

And this your heave offering shall be reckoned unto you, as though it were the corn of the threshing floor, and as the fullness of the winepress. (Numbers 18:27)

The tenth of tithes, a part (heave) of the offering offered of the tithe of the children of Israel belonged to the Levites.

TITHES AND OFFERINGS TO THE PEOPLE

There were tithes and offerings that were to be eaten by those who brought them: The people of God, the widow, the fatherless, the stranger, their menservants, and maidservants. The tithe of corn, wine, oil, the firstling of the herds of flocks and the increase of their seeds were to be eaten in a place, which God chose. Even their vows and freewill offerings were to be eaten by people who brought them.

Thou mayest not eat within thy gates the tithe of thy corn, or of thy wine, or of thy oil, or the firstlings of thy herds or of thy flock, nor any of thy vows which thou vowest, nor thy freewill offerings, or heave offering of thine hand: But thou must eat them before the LORD thy God in the place which the LORD thy God shall choose, thou, and thy son, and thy daughter, and thy manservant, and thy maidservant, and the Levite that

*is within thy gates: and thou shalt rejoice before the LORD
thy God in all that thou puttest thine hands unto. Take heed to
thyself that thou forsake not the Levite as long as thou livest
upon the earth. (Deuteronomy 12:17–19)*

*Thou shalt truly tithe all the increase of thy seed, that the
field bringeth forth year by year. And thou shalt eat before the
LORD thy God, in the place which he shall choose to place
his name there, the tithe of thy corn, of thy wine, and of thine
oil, and the firstlings of the herds and of thy flocks; that thou
mayest learn to fear the LORD thy God always. And if the way
be too long for thee, so that thou art not able to carry it; or if
the place be too far from thee, which the LORD thy God shall
choose to set his name there, when the LORD thy God hath
blessed thee: Then shalt thou turn it into money, and bind up
the money in thine hand, and shalt go unto the place which
the LORD thy God shall choose: And thou shalt bestow that
money for whatsoever thy soul lusteth after, for oxen, or for
sheep, or for wine, or for strong drink, or for whatsoever thy
soul desireth: and thou shalt eat there before the LORD thy
God, and thou shalt rejoice, thou, and thine household, And
the Levite that is within thy gates; thou shalt not forsake him;
for he hath no part nor inheritance with thee. At the end of
three years thou shalt bring forth all the tithe of thine increase
the same year, and shalt lay it up within thy gates: And the
Levite, (because he hath no part nor inheritance with thee,)
and the stranger, and the fatherless, and the widow, which are
within thy gates, shall come, and shall eat and be satisfied;
that the LORD thy God may bless thee in all the work of thine
hand which thou doest. (Deuteronomy 14:22–29)*

This portion of the Bible is clear. The people of Israel
brought their tithes year by year to the place that God chose.
The tithes were not to be eaten anywhere else. If the tithes

were too heavy to carry, the monetary equivalent was taken to the place God chose and there, it was bestowed on anything desired, even for strong drink. The tithes were eaten by the tithe payer's household, the Levites, the fatherless, the widow, and the stranger (visitors) in the house of God.

Every three years, the tithe payer invited the same group of people to their homes to eat together the tithe for the year. God is a God of faithfulness and without injustice! He did not talk to Abraham about tithing. When He did with Moses, He made provision for all in His house. Everybody was entitled to meat in the House of God.

What we hear from most pulpits is "Bring your tithe and offerings". However, we do not hear of any calling members to take of tithe and offering. It is preached that it is sacred and untouchable. Banks have become the Holies of Holies sanctified to warehouse this sacred offering and only those in business deserve to reap of the benefits of it.

If tithes and offerings belonged to God like they say, the Bible does show us the way to offer a sacrifice unto God: we must set them on fire! The tithe must be burnt to produce the sweet aroma that reaches God, then is it wholly God's. Whatever is not burnt belongs to all members of God's House: the Priest, the Levites, and the people according to the scriptures.

While the church has retained the tradition of receiving tithes and offerings, the tradition of making meat available in the house of God has been neglected as though it does not even exist. If the people of God have an obligation to bring their tithes and offering, then the leaders of the church have an obligation toward God to administer it the way He has commanded.

The Law does not just call for the tithing of our incomes; it calls for the tithing of our firstborn and for the tithing of our lands. The righteousness of the law is in the doing not in parts but completely. If the church must take tithes of income, then they should also call for our lands and children!

Therefore, if the ordinances of the Sabbath, burnt offering, circumcision, and tithe all dated back to the days of conscience, to the Law and the Prophets, and the Church claims that the sacrifice of the Lamb of God abolished them, then it should make spiritual sense that the same sacrifice on the cross abolished the ordinance of tithes and offerings. However, if the church decides to adopt the doctrine of receiving tithes from God's people, then the church is bond to the doctrine of disbursing tithe and offering: Some of the tithe should go to God. This is given to the priest Aaron. Some should go to the Levites who are the workers in the church. A portion must go to the people who bring in the tithe including the widow, the fatherless, and the stranger in the church.

Chapter Three

TITHE AND OFFERING AS IT AFFECTED THE STRUCTURE OF THE SANCTUARY

There was a structure in the House of God. According to the structure, God gave commandment concerning the allocation of all tithes, offerings, gifts, freewill offerings, and vows that were brought to the sanctuary by God's people. The sanctuary being God's family, made up of the Priest, the Levites and the people, the good Heavenly Father in His Words gave each and everyone in the house a portion of the meat in the house.

And I, behold, I have taken your brethren the Levites from among the children of Israel: to you they are given as a gift for the LORD, to do the service of the tabernacle of the congregation. Therefore thou and thy sons with thee shall keep your priest's office for every thing of the altar, and within the veil; and ye shall serve: I have given your priest's office unto you as a service of gift: and the stranger that cometh nigh shall be put to death. And the LORD spake unto Aaron, Behold, I also have given thee the charge of mine heave offerings of all the hallowed things of the children of Israel; unto thee have I given them by reason of the anointing, and to thy sons, by an ordinance for ever. This shall be thine of the most holy things, reserved from the fire: every oblation of theirs, every meat offering of theirs and every sin offering of theirs, and every trespass offering of theirs, which shall render unto me, shall be most holy for thee and for thy sons. In the most holy place shalt thou eat it; every male shall eat it: it shall be holy unto thee. (Numbers 18:6–10)

At the head of the structure in the sanctuary, were Aaron and his sons as priests. To them God gave the priest office as a Service of Gift. With this office came the charge of all holy things reserved from fire: every offering of the people, every meat offering, and every sin offering and every trespass offering that was not burnt; the tenth of all tithes, the wave offering, and the first fruits of their corn, wine, and oil were the priests'.

Following the priests of the sanctuary, were the Levites. Of the Levites, God charged Moses and Aaron:

And thy brethren also of the tribe of Levi, the tribe of thy father, bring thou with thee, that they may be joined unto thee, and minister unto thee: but thou and thy sons with thee shall minister before the tabernacle of witness. (Numbers 18:2)

And I, behold, I have taken your brethren the Levites from among the children of Israel: to you they are given as a gift for the LORD, to do the service of the tabernacle of the congregation. (Numbers 18:6)

"And, behold, I have given the children of Levi all the tenth in Israel for an inheritance, for their service, which they serve, even the service of the tabernacle of the congregation." (Numbers 18:21)

But the tithes of the children of Israel, which they offer as an heave offering unto the LORD, I have given to the Levites to inherit: therefore I have said unto them, Among the children of Israel they shall have no inheritance. (Numbers 18:24)

Thus speak unto the Levites, and say unto them, When ye take of the children of Israel the tithes which I have given you from them for your inheritance, then ye shall offer up an heave offering of it for the LORD, even a tenth part of the tithe. And this your heave offering shall be reckoned unto you, as though it were the corn of the threshing floor, and as the fullness of the winepress. Thus ye also shall offer an heave offering unto the LORD of all your tithes, which ye receive of the children of Israel; and ye shall give thereof the LORD'S heave offering to Aaron the priest. (Numbers 18:26–28)

The Levites ministered to the priests. The part of tithes offered as heave offerings belonged to the Levites who in turn offered a heave offering unto God. The heave offering unto God was given to Aaron and his sons who made up the priests' office. A tenth part of every tithe to the sanctuary also belonged to the Levites.

Following the Levites were the people. To the people who brought the tithes and offerings, God commanded:

Thou shalt truly tithe all the increase of thy seed, that the field bringeth forth year by year. And thou shalt eat before the LORD thy God, in the place which he shall choose to place his name there, the tithe of thy corn, of thy wine, and of thine oil, and the firstlings of the herds and of thy flocks; that thou mayest learn to fear the LORD thy God always. And if the way be too long for thee, so that thou art not able to carry it; or if the place be too far from thee, which the LORD thy God shall choose to set his name there, when the LORD thy God hath blessed thee: Then shalt thou turn it into money, and bind up the money in thine hand, and shalt go unto the place which the LORD thy God shall choose: And thou shalt bestow that money for whatsoever thy soul lusteth after, for oxen, or for sheep, or for wine, or for strong drink, or for whatsoever thy soul desireth: and thou shalt eat there before the LORD thy God, and thou shalt rejoice, thou, and

thine household, And the Levite that is within thy gates; thou shalt not forsake him; for he hath no part nor inheritance with thee. At the end of three years thou shalt bring forth all the tithe of thine increase the same year, and shalt lay it up within thy gates: And the Levite, (because he hath no part nor inheritance with thee,) and the stranger, and the father-less, and the widow, which are within thy gates, shall come, and shall eat and be satisfied; that the LORD thy God may bless thee in all the work of thine hand which thou doest.
(Deuteronomy 14:22–29)

Such was the structure laid by God in His House: The people brought the tithes and offerings to God's House, the Levites took a heave (a tenth or part of) offering of the people's tithes, and Aaron got a heave of the heave to the Levites. Whatever remained of the tithes and offerings belonged to the household of those who brought them, the stranger, the fatherless, and the widow in God's House.

That was in the Old Testament! The priest came from Aaron's family, the workers from one tribe - the tribe of Levi, and the people from one Nation - Israel. The church is of the New Testament and we have several churches each with an Aaron with different titles as President, Overseer, Pope, or Archbishop.

Following the Aarons of these churches are the Levites with names as Branch Pastors, Chapter Pastors and Deacons. All church workers that offer service to the Lord fall in the category of the Levites. Following the Levites are God's people.

It is commonplace to find tithes and offerings mostly in form of cash from a ministry going to the Aarons. This is because they believe that God has ordained that all that come to the sanctuary should go to the priests. The Aarons decide the fate of the remaining two categories of God's family.

For some Aarons, if God has called the Levites, the Levites should prove so by their total dependence on God for their own sustenance: They should live by faith or work out their own "breakthrough." The proof of God's calling on a man's life has come to be measured on how much material things he is blessed with.

We have situations where offerings from the branches are all sent to what they call "Headquarters." According to these Aarons, they are hallowed, sanctified, and untouchable even by the Levites.

Branch Pastors, let alone members of churches are not allowed access to these accounts even if the money were meant to do God's business like getting a place of worship. The funds for God's business must be raised from God's people any time there is a need to do God's business in spite of millions raised and stashed away in the banks.

The Bible declares that every believer has been made king and priest unto God with Christ as the only High Priest (Revelation 1:5). This invariably entitles the Christian to the benefits of priesthood. If the tradition of tithing is according to God's Word, then the tradition of eating or sharing it must be obeyed. Then is it righteousness and judgment for the present day church to call on God's people to bring their tithes and offerings.

The people that bring tithes are entitled to the tithe. In fact, most part of the tithe is theirs for the eating. A tenth of the tithe belongs to workers or helpers in the ministry and a tenth of what goes to the workers goes to the Aaron - Presidents or Overseers or Archbishops or Popes.

To understand what part belongs to the Aaron and the Levites, we would consider some kinds of offerings - The Wave Offering, the Heave Offering, and the First-fruits.

WAVE OFFERING

Also thou shalt take of the ram the fat and the rump and the fat that covereth the inwards, and the caul above the liver, and the two kidneys, and the fat that is upon them, and the right shoulder; for it is a ram of consecration: And one loaf of bread, and one cake of oiled bread, and one wafer out of the basket of the unleavened bread that is before the LORD: And thou shalt put all in the hands of Aaron, and in the hands of his sons; and shalt wave them for a wave offering before the LORD. (Exodus 29:22–24)

A wave offering is a collection of parts of an offering that the priest waves before God. In the offering described above, the fat of the ram, the caul, the two kidneys, the right shoulders, a loaf of bread, one cake of oiled bread and a wafer of unleavened bread were waved as a wave offering unto God.

In the offering described below, the breast was offered as a wave offering.

His own hands shall bring the offerings of the LORD made by fire, the fat with the breast, it shall he bring, that the breast may be waved for a wave offering before the LORD. And the priest shall burn the fat upon the altar: but the breast shall be Aaron's and his sons'. (Leviticus 7:30–31)

HEAVE OFFERING

The heave of an offering is a part of the offering. For instance, the right shoulder of a ram offered is the heave offering from that sacrifice. This forms part of the wave offering and belongs to the priest who offers the sacrifice for the people.

And the right shoulder shall ye give unto the priest for a heave offering of the sacrifices of your peace offerings. He among the sons of Aaron, that offereth the blood of the peace offerings, and the fat, shall have the right shoulder for his part. For the wave breast and the heave shoulder have I taken of the children of Israel from off the sacrifices of their peace offerings, and have given them unto Aaron the priest and unto his sons by a statute for ever from among the children of Israel. This is the portion of the anointing of Aaron, and of the anointing of his sons, out of the offerings of the LORD made by fire, in the day when he presented them to minister unto the LORD in the priest's office; (Leviticus 7:32–35)

Heaves of all hallowed offerings belong to the priests (Numbers 18:8). Heave of tithes brought in by the people belongs to the Levites (Numbers 18:24) who in turn offer a heave unto Aaron (Numbers 18:28)

THE FEAST OF FIRST-FRUITS

First-fruits is a feast observed by the Israelites: It is the feast of harvest. It is one of the three feasts the children of Israel were commanded to observe every year.

Three times thou shalt keep a feast unto me in the year. Thou shalt keep the feast of unleavened bread: (thou shalt eat unleavened bread seven days, as I commanded thee, in the time appointed of the month Abib; for in it thou camest out from Egypt: and none shall appear before me empty:) And the feast of harvest, the firstfruits of thy labours, which thou hast sown in the field: and the feast of ingathering, which is in the end of the year, when thou hast gathered in thy labours out of the field. (Exodus 23:14–16)

"The first of the firstfruits of thy land thou shalt bring into the house of the LORD thy God . . ." (Exodus 23:19)

The feast and the first-fruits are described in the verses below.

And the LORD spake unto Moses, saying, Speak unto the children of Israel, and say unto them, When ye be come into the land which I give unto you, and shall reap the harvest thereof, then ye shall bring a sheaf of the firstfruits of your harvest unto the priest: And he shall wave the sheaf before the LORD, to be accepted for you: on the morrow after the sabbath the priest shall wave it. And ye shall offer that day when ye wave the sheaf an he lamb without blemish of the first year for a burnt offering unto the LORD. And the meat offering thereof shall be two tenth deals of fine flour mingled with oil, an offering made by fire unto the LORD for a sweet savour: and the drink offering thereof shall be of wine, the fourth part of an hin. And ye shall eat neither bread, nor parched corn, nor green ears, until the selfsame day that ye have brought an offering unto your God: it shall be a statute for ever throughout your generations in all your dwellings. And ye shall count unto you from the morrow after the sabbath, from the day that ye brought the sheaf of the wave offering; seven sabbaths shall be complete: Even unto the morrow after the seventh Sabbath shall ye number fifty days; and ye shall offer a new meat offering unto the LORD. Ye shall bring out of your habitations two wave loaves of two tenth deals: they shall be of fine flour; they shall be baken with leaven; they are the first-fruits unto the LORD . . .
(Leviticus 23:9–20)

During the feast of First Fruits, the people of Israel brought the first fruit or the first bundle from the first harvest accompanied with some other items to the priest who waved them before God. For instance, if one plants a grape vine, the first and one bunch of grape fruits plucked from any grape tree is the first fruit. The people of Israel set this bunch apart from the rest of the bunches of grapes harvested on that same day and brought the one bunch of grapes to the priest to wave it before the Lord. Fifty days later, two loaves of fine flour baked with leaven is offered with lambs, one young bullock, and rams as burnt offering to the Lord. It is a feast full of ceremonies. However, the two loaves of fine flour represents the *first-fruits* unto God.

The doctrine of first-fruits is recently gaining ground in churches. Some preach that it is the first income received in the first month of each year; some others say it is the first increment on income in the year. It is clear from God's Word that it is not just about bringing money; there are ceremonies to be observed, rams and goats to be slaughtered, and bread to be baked to make it the first-fruits God commanded. It is a feast!

If the church is particular about observing this feast, then it should be ready to observe all other feasts like the Sabbath (Leviticus 23:1–3), the Passover ((Leviticus 23:5), the unleavened bread (Leviticus 23:6), the feast of ingathering, the feast of tabernacles and several other feasts. The feast of tabernacles for instance, is a feast that would be observed through out all generations. The Bible reveals that when the old heaven and earth disappear and Jesus Christ reigns as King on the new earth, every nation would have to go to Jerusalem to observe the feast of tabernacles (Zechariah 14:16).

Did God not call for the observance of three feasts in Exodus 23:14? So why has the present day church singled out just the first-fruits? This is not righteous and neither is it obedience. The church observes the feast of first-fruits; the church becomes a debtor to observe other feasts.

If the church must go back to the law of the spirit of death, then the church must be ready to bring all to bear, not partly.

Chapter Four

Spurious Teachings of Giving

Many preachers, with the intent to incite fear so that Christians continually live in condemnation of heart, tailor the Word of God to communicate a particular idea, a process that sometimes results in the preacher citing a particular verse of scripture out of context. Pastors have many doctrines on giving. However, some of these doctrines, which have a form of spirituality, have their roots from demonic worship as Pastors compare the giving to God to giving to idols. They would tell how anyone visiting to consult an oracle would first have to drop money before the idols would attend to their request. By this association, they would explain that God deserves more of such worship than the idols. It is irking to hear them make such comparison because none of the doctrines has any scriptural basis: They exalt themselves against the knowledge of God's Word and should be brought low.

The Bible warned against the introduction of heretical doctrines in the church and against many who will in their lust for wealth; exploit the church with false arguments. Any teaching that tends to shift the focus of the Christian from the work of the sacrifice of Jesus Christ on the cross to turn them to the power in the sacrifice of mammon is damnable heresy (2 Peter 2:1–3).

Borrowing to Give

The message of working out our salvation has been turned away from faith, hope, love, the studying of the Word, from prayers, evangelism and the unity of faith to the giving of tithes and offerings. Announcement of money that members give is made in church services even when Jesus Christ taught that the left hand should not know what the right is giving. Tithe cards are printed to record names of tithe payers, and registers are opened to give details. It is even being recorded electronically for some churches and except one is a tithe payer, one is considered not saved or not entitled to the brotherly love the Bible exhorts Christians to share as brethren. When the needy come to church to complain of lack, the needy are told to borrow and sow to frustrate the devil and poverty. We read of Elisha instructing a certain woman of the wives of the sons of the prophets to borrow more vessels, but they were for him to fill with the oil that would flow from her small pot of oil He did not request the widow to borrow oil for him to bless.

We find brethren borrowing from other brethren to give as seeds, only for the creditor to come asking and be denied repayment because the harvest hoped for is yet to happen. I heard a man of God preaching on the incident of Elijah and the prophets of Baal. According to him, though there was drought in the land of Israel, Elijah had requested that twelve barrels of water be brought and poured on the sacrifice that he had prepared. God answered Elijah and sent fire from heaven to leak the water and consume the sacrifice because Elijah gave God what was lacking in the nation of Israel. According to him, though there was no water in the land, yet Elijah offered twelve barrels of water and for that reason God answered him with fire. The preacher rounded up by proclaiming, "If you want God in action, give to Him what is lacking to get what you want." Yet, verse one of that chapter had read, "And it came to pass after many days, that the word of the LORD came to Elijah in the third year, saying, Go, shew thyself unto Ahab; and I will send rain upon the earth." (1 Kings 18:1)

Elijah had ceased rain for three and half years. God spoke to Elijah before the expiry of the three and half years because God was eager to give the land rain. He told Elijah to go show himself to Ahab. God did not send Elijah to make him a sacrifice to enable him to send rain, but He instructed him to show himself to the king. Why would it be correct to teach that God gave rain because of Elijah's sacrifice? This is the kind of teaching taught in some churches with respect to giving - the story of God answering by fire and sending rain because God was given twelve barrels of water in time of drought or give to God what you do not have to get what you want.

It is biblical to give, and give the very last of what we have in love and willingly. However, there is no one in the scriptures that gave what he or she did not have. Everyone, whoever gave, gave of what God had blessed him or her. King David who said he would not give to the Lord that which cost him nothing gave out of abundance; Solomon offered sacrifices out of abundance; Jacob gave from abundance; Abraham was willing to give his only son Isaac, and the widow gave the last she had. No one borrowed to give to God. Hannah made a vow to give back to God if He gave to her. Giving what is not ours as offering to God is wrong! Borrowing to give is not scriptural.

The Bible has no record of anyone giving to God because they wanted to be rich. Not Abel, Abraham, Isaac, nor David. Not even Paul. Everyone who gave did so in honor and respect for the relationship they shared with God. The Bible gave the secret to prosperity, "By humility and fear of the LORD are riches, and honor and life." (Proverb 22:4)

SOWING TO THE ANOINTING

Believers are asked to sow into a minister's anointing. According to the doctrine, if one desires to operate in the same anointing as some pastor, what is required is to keep sowing to the pastor by giving gifts to him. This doctrine, in spite of the scriptural face it wears, only reminds me of the incident between Peter and Simon - the sorcerer.

And when Simon saw that through laying on of the apostles' hands the Holy Ghost was given, he offered them money, asses, six thousand seven hundred and twenty saying, Give me also this power, that on whomsoever I lay hands, he may receive the Holy Ghost. But Peter said unto him, Thy money perish with thee, because thou hast thought that the gift of God may be purchased with money. (Acts 8:18–20)

In Peter's case, Simon offered money willingly, but these days, it is the pastor offering the anointing for the gift. The anointing is the gift of God and cannot be purchased by money or gifts. Jesus Christ taught in the following scripture the grounds on which our giving is rewarded.

He that receiveth a prophet in the name of a prophet shall receive a prophet's reward; and he that receiveth a righteous man in the name of a righteous man shall receive a righteous man's reward. And whosoever shall give to drink unto one of these little ones a cup of cold water only in the name of a disciple, verily I say unto you, he shall in no wise lose his reward. (Matthew 10:41–42)

If we give a prophet our money because he is a prophet, we will get a prophet's reward. This means that the reward lies with the prophet. Jesus Christ did not tell us what a prophet's reward would be. It means the one who gives to a prophet because he is a prophet should not expect any reward from heaven. Our giving will be rewarded by heaven if we give someone a cup of water in the Name of Jesus

Christ. We will only be rewarded for things we do as if Jesus Christ did them.

Some great men of God who were given gifts rejected them—Abraham would not even take the goods from the cause that he had fought and won; Elisha would not accept Naaman's gift; David would not accept a land willingly given him for sacrifice to his God, and the Apostle Paul is a prime New Testament example. Coming from Syria to Israel to be healed of leprosy by Elisha, Naaman took with him gifts for the prophet, ten talents of silver, and six thousand pieces of gold, and ten changes of raiment. In appreciation for his healing, Naaman offered gifts to Elisha. Even when persuaded, Elisha would take no gift of Naaman. Nevertheless, Ghazi, Elisa's servant thought differently. He went after Naaman for the gifts. He paid for it!

The anointing is not any Pastor's to give away to anybody he chooses. When the mother of James and John - the sons of Zebedee came to Jesus Christ and requested that Jesus Christ grant them to sit on the left and right hand in His glory, Jesus Christ made it clear that it was not in His power to grant (Matthew 10:35–40). Even so, the anointing is God's to give to anyone He chooses.

The giving to the pastors therefore should be done in love to meet needs in their lives just like the early church ministered to Paul, not to sow into his anointing. God's anointing comes with knowledge and the Holy Ghost. It is a gift freely given of God.

As Peter counseled Simon, the pastor that believes that he can transfer the anointing for gifts has neither part nor share in the matter.

You have neither part nor lot in this matter, for your heart is not right in the sight of God. Repent therefore of this thy wickedness, and pray God, if perhaps the thought of thine heart may be forgiven thee. For I perceive that thou art in a gall of bitterness, and in the bond of iniquity. (Acts 8:21–22)

Sowing for Healing and Deliverance

Christians are often advised by some preachers to sow a seed for their deliverance, some for healing and others for one miracle or the other. The Lord Jesus Christ must be heart-broken in heaven! How could He have gone through so much pain and shame for man; to be wounded for man's transgression, bruised for their iniquity beaten beyond recognition for their healing, lived poor so that they could be rich (Isaiah 53:4–5), only for the same people to trust more in the power of mammon than in His sacrifice! What a huge waste! But the scripture lets us know that God that spared not His own Son, but delivered Him up for us all, shall with Him also freely give us all things (Romans 8:32–34). For we have received, not the spirit of the world, but the spirit which is of God; that we might know the things that are freely given to us of God.

All things include all things that would enable us live a good and godly life. All that we require to do is know, understand and accept that all things have been freely given of God in Jesus Christ. If God gave Jesus Christ without our asking, giving and contribution, why do we have to give Him money to have Him do anything for us?

Jesus Christ said to everyone that came to him, "According to your faith be it unto you" (Mathew 9:29) or "**Thy faith** hath made thee whole" (Mark 10:52). No one gave to Him to be forgiven, healed, delivered, or blessed. Why would God who freely offered His own Son for us, not freely give us all things? Our deliverance, salvation, health, wealth, joy, and peace were embedded in the sacrifice of the cross. If we have to give money to God to be healed, blessed or forgiven, then Jesus Christ died in vain!

The Bible admonishes Christians to put on the whole armor of God. This armor does not include giving to ward off fiery darts of the enemy. It is made up of truth as our waist belt; righteousness as our breastplate and the preparation for the gospel of peace for our shoes. With the helmet of salvation on our heads, faith should be our shield against all the sharp arrows of the wicked. The Word of God that we speak in every circumstance is our sword of the Spirit. Persevering in prayers and supplication in the spirit for all saints is to be the daily life of a Christian.

If we must give our lands or houses or cars or money, our all, we must learn to give in love to meet a need, not because we expect God to do something because of the money we think we have given Him. The only price worthy has been paid. God sure does not need our money. What need our money are the needs around us.

If a Christian is sick and desires healing, the only right he or she has to be healed is because Jesus Christ paid for the healing as the Bible witnesses that by His stripes we were healed (Isaiah 53:5). The only right we have to be rich is because the Bibles witnesses that He became poor so that by his poverty we become rich, not because we gave God some money. I wonder how He feels when we do what we do.

CONNECTING TO THE WORD

Jesus Christ said to his disciples, "Heal the sick, cleanse the lepers, raise the dead, cast out devils: freely ye have received, freely give." (Matthew 10:8–9.) However, it is not so anymore as brethren would have to give an offering before a minister can pray and bless God's people. They say it is a way of connecting to the blessing. Some of God's ministers have decided like Gehazi, that they cannot let go the gifts and have devised scriptural logics to support the disobedience of the counsel from the Lord Jesus Christ.

Therefore, we find brethren filing out during the ministration of the Word to drop money on the altar to connect to a blessing in the message. According to this teaching, when this is done, you are certain that the blessing in the message preached will produce results proclaimed in the message. I cannot tell what it is but I do know that no such foundation was laid in the scriptures. Jesus Christ did not do it; the apostles did not. I do not see the Holy Ghost teaching such doctrine in this dispensation of grace. Something must be wrong, and I suspect that the devil has devised a way to erode faith in Jesus Christ from the heart of the Christian to turn them to their works, and the church ought to be warned. For no other foundation must be established except Jesus Christ and Him crucified.

As far as I am concerned, the teaching that Christians drop money on the altar while a message is been preached or before prayers are said is tantamount to retailing the anointing. I see it as a method to get paid for the hours preachers spend studying and praying before the service. The preacher would have prayed for the manifestation of God's presence during the service; so when the congregation begins to feel the manifestation of that presence by the good and skilled oratory, the preacher thinks the congregation should pay to have God's Word work for them. This doctrine, though having a show of humility is also not scriptural. There is no record of anyone in scriptures giving money or anything to connect to God's Word.

Giving money on the altar to connect to the Word completely negates the issue of faith in God's Word and this is confusing when compared to what Jesus preached and the way He lived. So countless are the messages preached to collect money from members that it is as if God has placed a handsome reward on the best collector. The parable of the faithful servants does not seem to help this situation as the Lord is portrayed to be pleased with the stewards who through trading doubled the talents given them. Therefore, the preachers are trading with the anointing to obtain praise from their master.

Like the prophet in the drama, some rule over the people to collect all that they have. Their vision must come to pass whether it is God-driven or it is self-driven: So they go right back into scriptures and dig up some abolished traditions, like first-fruits, sin offering, peace offering and so on. When it comes to some doctrines, they are the church of the New Testament: Then the law is abolished. But when it comes to giving, they become the church of the Old Testament. The children of God must tithe or face the devourer.

As long as pastors continue to judge God's people in tithes and offerings, circumcision, first-fruits and every other matters of the law, then they make Christ of no effect, and then the Church has fallen from grace!

It is the responsibility of God's children to take care of His vineyard. It will be irresponsible for a Christian to watch and wait until he or she is pushed or cajoled to give toward the expansion of God's kingdom. As Christians, we have the responsibility to build places of worship; sponsor His crusade to evangelize the world, take care of His pastors and very importantly, to take care of the weak and needy in His house. God does not only deserve a tenth of our lives, he is worthy of our all.

Who would in a relationship have respect for a partner or friend if all he does were to expect a reward for every little thing he does? Such a relationship is no longer based on love, but on gains. And as Christians if all we do is give to God so that He can double or give back to us, then are we yet without honor and integrity, and indeed poor specimen of what the Sons of God should be, far from the hopes and dreams of Jesus Christ when he submitted himself to be bruised for our sins.

Which of us expect rewards when we clean up our houses, do the laundries, cut the grass, and prepare meals? Who craves payment for being a father or a mother or a son or daughter? In the same vein, Christians should look away from rewards that come from giving, and give because it is the Christian's nature and responsibility to give, not just money, but everything. Jesus taught us to give and not expect reward.

In church, we find that everyone who cleans the church does it to buy favor from God; those who go for evangelism do so to get a blessing. It is reward, reward, and reward! If we get paid for everything we do, what reward do we then expect when we stand before God in glory? Bible called the Christian a co-laborer, not for God, but with God! Why should we expect Him to pay us when we labor with him to win souls, feed his flocks, or build a worship place?

However, just like the law of the force of gravity, there is the law of sowing and reaping: For as long as the heaven and the earth remain, seedtime and harvest, cold and heat, summer and winter, day and night shall not cease (Gen 8:22). Therefore, we always reap the harvest of what we sow, and it is more blessed to give than to receive, the one who gives also should receive. The immutability of these laws cannot be over emphasized. Yet the way and manner this message is delivered is becoming terrifying and pastors must exercise caution.

It is heresy to single out tithe, offerings, and first-fruits out of tens of laws that have been abolished (2 Corinthians 3:13), and consider it righteousness to bring God's people under the curse of the devourer after the price Jesus Christ paid to redeem the church from the curse of the law (Galatians 3:13).

Chapter Five

It is interesting to know that when the Lord Jesus Christ spoke on the subject tithing, it was not to eulogize those who pay tithes, but to rebuke them. It was "woe" to them that would tithe of salt and onions but would not turn in mercy in the way of brethren in need.

Woe to you, Scribes and Pharisee, hypocrite! For you tithe mint and dill and cummin, and have neglected the weightier matters of the law, justice and mercy and faith; these you ought to have done, without neglecting others. (Matthew 23:23)

To Jesus Christ, it was hypocrisy bringing the tithes while forsaking justice, mercy, and faith toward God and man. Jesus Christ associated tithing not with Abraham but with the law; He classified tithing under the lesser matter of the Law while justice, mercy, and faith were weightier matters in the Law.

Jesus Christ's categorization of tithing as of the Law undoubtedly should eliminate the theology that defends the tradition of tithing in the church based on the church's relationship with Abraham. As far as the Lord of Life is concerned, it is of the Law of Moses to tithe.

In His teachings, He taught that man was not made for the Law but Law for man. He worked on Sabbath day (Mark 2:23–28). He would eat with His hands unwashed; He associated with tax collectors and adulterers. He did not see any man the way human or the Law saw them, but the way God's grace saw them. Life in Christianity would be heavenly if only pastors can see the flocks of God the way God's grace sees them.

Jesus Christ did a lot of good works: "For God anointed Jesus Christ of Nazareth with the Holy Ghost and with power: who went about doing good, and healing all that was oppressed of the devil; for God was with Him (Acts 10:38). Jesus Christ's goodness was not just in teaching kingdom principles, healing and working miracles, He identified with the poor and gave to them from the purse of His ministry. His disciples testified to this.

For some of them thought, because Judas had the bag, that Jesus Christ has said unto him, buy those things that we have need of against the feast; or that he should give something to the poor.(John 13:29)

Jesus Christ is the Word of God made manifest in the flesh, the light of the world. Yet, when He met the poor, He would not teach on the principles of giving and receiving. He gave as much as was in His power to meet the needs of the poor. When he entered the world, He said, "Sacrifices and offerings You have not desired, but instead You have made ready a body for Me [to offer]" (Hebrew 10:5–6, TAB). When Jesus Christ offered up his body, it was a once-for-all-sacrifice. If Jesus Christ is the perfect sacrifice and offering, to what purpose are the offerings and sacrifices of various forms called for in the church today? It was shocking to hear a Christian testify to receiving answers to prayers after carrying out a sacrifice of money. That was the extreme: Christians having to carry out sacrifices after all that Jesus Christ had done for them. It is sad!

It is important to note that though these practices of sowing seeds and sacrificing money to receive healing or prosperity seem to produce results for the people that do them, judging from the testimonies we hear, that does not make these doctrines God's will and intent for His Church. When Moses struck the rock a second time instead of speaking to it as God had instructed, water flowed from it even though God's instruction was disregarded. That there was water for the children of Israel to drink did not make Moses' action justifiable before God. The same could be said for some of the doctrines taught in God's Church these days. The doctrine of calling for tithe and offering, first fruits, sacrifices of money as the gateway to God's blessing may seem to yield results, but they do not represent God's intentions in a dispensation of Grace.

Jesus Christ rebuking the Scribes and Pharisee said, " . . . Thus have ye made the commandment of God of none effect by your tradition" (Matthew 15:6). The church is doing just the same. Grace says we are healed by the stripes of Jesus Christ, but the pastors say if you are sick and cannot get well, drop money on the altar and you will be well. Grace says we are made rich by Christ's poverty, but the Pastors says keep giving and you would be rich. Then brethren begin to file out to tell how they did it and it worked. This relegates the sacrifice of Jesus Christ to the background; it is made of no effect in the life of the Christian. When a Christian falls sick, the first intuition becomes to give an offering. This is not good! Sowing to be healed, sowing to be delivered, sowing to connect to an anointing, sowing to have the Word productive, sowing to get rich, tithing for fear of the devourer are not traditions associated with grace.

Christians who live by one aspect of the law are obliged to keep the whole law because the keeping of the law nullifies the grace of Jesus Christ. The church cannot be in between the two - the Law and Grace. The presence of one signifies the absence of the other. We cannot confess to being

saved by Grace only to live our lives based on the Law. The presence of the Law nullifies Grace!

Paul, admonishing the Christian wrote:

For I testify again to every man that is circumcised, that he is a debtor to do the whole law. Christ is become of effect unto you, whosoever of you are justified by the law; ye are fallen from grace. (Galatians 5:3–4)

He distinguished between the righteousness that is of the Law, the righteousness that is of God and the righteousness that is of man (self-righteousness). In his letter to the Romans, Paul wrote:

Now we know that what thing so ever the law saith, it saith to them who are under the law: that every mouth may be stopped, and all the world may become guilty before God. Therefore by the deeds of the law there shall no flesh be justified in his sight: for by the law is the knowledge of sin. But now the righteousness of God without the law is manifested, being witnessed by the law and the prophets; even the righteousness of God which is by faith of Jesus Christ unto all and upon all them that believe. (Roman 3:19–22)

What shall we say then that Abraham our father, as pertaining to the flesh, hath found? For if Abraham were justified by works, he hath whereof to glory; but not before God. For what saith the scriptures? Abraham believed God, and it was counted unto him for righteousness. (Romans 4:1–3)

For the promise, that he should be heir of the world, was not to Abraham, or to his seed, through the law, but through the righteousness of faith. For if they which are of the law be heirs, faith is made void, and the promise made of no effect:

Because the law worketh wrath, for where no law is, there is no transgression. Therefore it is of faith, that it might be by grace; to the end the promise might be sure to all the seed; not to that only which is of the law, but to that also which is of the faith of Abraham; who is the father of us all. (Romans 4:13–16)

Whether tithe is of Abraham or of the law, Paul sought to clarify that the sons of God are saved by grace and not by any good work. Man can take the glory for good works but not before God. Just as a Christian is saved by the confession of faith in Jesus Christ (Romans 10:9), a Christian should be healed not because of some money sowed for health, but because the Bible witnesses that, we were healed by the stripes of Jesus (1 Peter 2:4). A Christian should be prosperous because Jesus became poor that through His poverty we might be rich (2 Corinthian 8:9). A Christian is righteous not because of the good works but because the Bible let us know that Jesus was made sin for us that we might become the righteousness of God in Him (2 Corinthians 5:21).

If we expect to be healed because of the money we give, it is no longer the righteousness of God at work, but our own righteousness. If we have to tithe so that God would open the windows of heaven and pour down a blessing, it is no longer the righteousness that is by Grace, but of the Law. "For Moses describeth the righteousness which is of the law, that the man which doeth those things shall live by them" (Roman 10:5).

Paul pointed out something else about the law. "The law worketh wrath." This should explain why some pastors do not mind handing over the flock of God over to sickness and various forms of calamity for destruction on failure to pay tithe and offering. They could get so angry with a member of the church whose name does not appear on the church tithe record so much that their hearts begin to wish that something terrible would befall him so that he would learn to give. This is the evidence of the Law at work.

Paul said of the Jews,

Brethren, my heart desire and prayer to God for Israel is that they might be saved. For I bear them record that they have the zeal of God, but not according to knowledge. For they being ignorant of God's righteousness', and going about to establish their own righteousness, have not submitted themselves unto the righteousness of God. For Christ is the end of the law for righteousness to everyone that believeth. (Romans 10:1–4)

The teaching that man must give to God to receive of Him is self-righteousness. Jesus described Him in Matthew 5:45 as the Father in heaven who makes the sun to shine on the evil and on the good. He does not expect anything for giving sunshine and rain. We do not have to give to God to get Him to gives us the flowers in their season. We do not give to have Him give night and the day. If He says He has freely given us all we need to live a good and godly life, we should take Him by His Word in any circumstance.

Righteousness was not imputed to Abraham because he gave tithe or his son Isaac, but because he believed God's Word to him. As for the law, Jesus Christ is the end of the law for righteousness to everyone that believes. When the Jews boasted of being Abraham's children, Jesus Christ was quick to correct that God could make children for Abraham from stones, and he said, " . . . Before Abraham was, I am" (John 8:58). This encapsulates that the intent to send Jesus Christ for the salvation of man was before Abraham, but God had chosen to fulfill the plan through Abraham just as He chose David to be king and Mary to be the mother of the Word of God. Jesus Christ therefore is the foundation of our salvation and the basis for traditions and doctrines in the church. The church should look unto Jesus Christ the author and finisher of our faith. It should not stand on any other, not even Abraham! How did Jesus Christ live, what did He teach, and what did he say about our day-to-day living? His life and example should be enough standards for the Church - His body.

Jesus Christ Teachings on Giving

Jesus Christ taught everyone to give. His counsel on giving should make enough sermons for any Pastor on giving.

Jesus Christ said, "Give, and it shall be give unto you; good measure, pressed down, and shaken together, and running over, shall men give into your bosom" (Luke 6:38). In Matthew 5:42, He taught us to, give to him that ask us and not to turn away any that would borrow of us. In Luke 6:34, Jesus Christ asked, "And if ye lend to them of whom ye hope to receive, what thank have ye? For sinners also lend to sinners, to receive as much again." And in verse thirty-five of the same chapter, he taught us to " . . . lend hoping for nothing again; and our reward shall be great, and we shall be the children of the highest: for he is kind unto the unthankful and to the evil."

On receiving He said, "Ask, and it shall be given you; seek, and ye shall find; knock, and it shall be opened unto you: For every one that asketh receiveth; and he that seeketh findeth; and to him that knocketh it shall be opened" (Matthew 7:7–8). Then He said, " . . . What thing so ever ye desire, we you pray, believe that you receive them and you shall have them" (Mark 11:24).

It is a long time since I heard anyone preach this gospel of asking and receiving. Sowing seeds to receive seems to have taken over this simple teaching of faith. Pastors even preach that sowing money is a way of seeking to find and knocking to have the door open. These doctrines would have been easier to accept if Jesus Christ taught them. But He did not! In John 14:13, Jesus said, "And whatsoever ye shall ask in my name, that will I do, that the Father may be glorified in the Son." If we had to give to have the Father hear us and answer us promptly, Jesus Christ would have told us. He made us know that the only reason we do not receive is that we do not ask the Father in his name. (John16: 23–24)

In Ephesians 6:8, Paul admonished, " . . . Whatsoever good thing any man doeth, the same shall he receive of the Lord, whether he be bond or free."

These scriptures are enough bases for Christians to give. The new creation should give because Jesus Christ teaches that it is more blessed to give than to receive. Jesus Christ never called on anyone to give to God, but He instructs us to give to anyone that asks us. He revealed that men will back to us in good measure, shaken together and running over if we will give to them that ask or borrow of us. Jesus Christ showed that whatever we do to any of the brethren, we did for Him (Matthew 25:40).

THE WAY THE NEW TESTAMENT SEES 'OFFERING'

In Mark 12:41 Jesus Christ stood by and watched people give money in the synagogue. The Bible did not see them as giving an offering to God, instead, the writer of the book of Mark was careful to use the phrase "cast money into the treasury." I believe that this act described in Mark 12:41 matches with what the Church calls giving offerings to God.

There is indeed a treasury in God's house that requires replenishing; when we give in church, it is to replenish the treasury and not as if we are offering a sacrifice to God. Jesus Christ entered the Holy of Holies and offered up Himself to God as the only acceptable offering and sacrifice once and for all! Jesus teaching in Matthew 5:24, referred to what is brought and offered on the altar as gifts.

I often hear Christians say; "I am a covenant child because I pay my tithe." The Bible did not say such things as tithing being a covenant because it is not. I have never heard or read of a spiritual covenant made between two people by bringing their money together or a covenant where one brings blood and the other brings money. No amount of money can be a match for the blood of the Son of God on the cross. Christians are in a covenant with Jesus Christ not because of their money but because of their professed faith in the shedding of His own blood. God did not require our blood or money as part of that sacrifice on the cross. I do not think He has changed His mind either.

It is wrong for anyone to place the bases of our covenant with God on money, the only covenant being the testament in the blood of Jesus Christ. Anything that distracts from the sacrifice of Jesus is sin!

Chapter Six

GIVING IN THE EARLY CHURCH
MINISTERING TO BRETHREN

The early church of the New Testament gave. This was the church that started on the day of Pentecost when cloven tongues as of fire came upon one hundred and twenty people that were gathered awaiting Jesus Christ's promise to endue them with power from on high. Three thousand people were saved and added to the church the same day. More were saved after. We could estimate the church in Jerusalem to be more than five thousand people. This indeed could be said to be very large number compared to the number of people we have seated in each church building on worship days. Yet, the early church gave to meet needs. To whom, for what and why did the early church give?

Neither was there any among them that lacked: for as many as were possessors of lands or houses sold them, and brought the prices of the things that were sold, And laid them down at the apostles' feet: and distribution was made unto every man according as he had need. And Joses, who by the apostles was surnamed Barnabas, (which is, being interpreted, The son of consolation,) a Levite, and of the country of Cyprus, Having land, sold it, and brought the money, and laid it at the apostles' feet (Acts 4:34–37)

The Bible explained that the Church was of one mind. We are also told that none lacked amongst the brethren, not because God blessed everyone with prosperity but because those who had possessions sold them and gave to those in need. The Bible did not tell us whether they were preached into selling their properties. I am compelled to believe they were. I can infer this from the episode of Ananias and Sapphira. I have wondered why they would have sold a land that was theirs, kept some part of the money, and lied about it. Why was Peter interested in whether they gave all or some part? Since the Bible said nothing about it, I have no answers to the question. Yet, there was an anointing on Peter, which judged these brethren speedily causing their death. The same Peter, who once denied the Lord of life and was forgiven without his asking, would not give these brethren a chance for repentance because he was angry.

Looking at Peter's action with the eyes of Jesus Christ, I would say this is not a right attitude of a shepherd toward God's sheep. Yet, such is the attitude of some pastors toward their sheep when it comes to money. They subtly make members choose between spending the money for the devil by having a loved one taking ill or have thieves break into them to steal. They would usually say, "Which one is better, give it to God or spend it in the hospital?" They would tell how a member suffered loss of health, property, or life because he would not give. They bring God's people under yokes for not giving. When a pastor, while preaching on giving, makes statements like "Which do you think is better, to give to God or to pay it to the hospital?" such a pastor is indirectly asking the congregation to choose between giving to God and falling sick. It is another way of handing the congregation over to Satan for destruction of their soul and body.

When the apostles called for giving in the early church, they gave so that no one lacked in the church. The proceeds from the possessions sold were not to tour the earth preaching the good news or build fine worship places, or buy state of the art cars or acquire more lands; it was first to meet the needs of the brethren so that no one lacked.

This aspect of ministry in the church is completely ignored when the message of giving is preached; some would argue that the communal fellowship that was possible with the early church is not workable in the society of the present generation. Yet, it is so easy to refer to ages past when it comes to asking the people to give.

The depth of the deception that could dwell in the heart of a shepherd toward the people he leads struck me when I listened to a pastor exhort brethren on Acts 4:34–35. He had read,

Neither was there any among them that lacked: for as many as were possessors of lands or houses sold them, and brought the prices of the things that were sold, and laid them down at the apostles' feet: and distribution was made unto every man according as he had need.

The preacher then pointed out to his audience that Christians of the church brought all the proceeds of the goods to the apostles' feet and left off saying anything on the distribution to the saints. He went on to read,

And Joses, who by the apostles was surnamed Barnabas, (which is being interpreted, The son of consolation) a Levite, and of the country of Cyprus, having land, sold it and brought the money and laid it at the apostles' feet.

Explaining this passage, the preacher told his audience, that the need of the brethren was so much in those days that there was not enough to preach the gospel. He added that Barnabas had sold his land and brought it to the Apostles to enable them preach the gospel. According to him, the money was so much that his name was mentioned in the Bible.

I was stunned because the preacher was a pastor of a

church that believed in giving. I perceived he was trying to answer the unasked questions he suspected would be in minds of his listeners - the flock of God under his care. The passages he had read said distribution was made to the brethren of what was brought to the apostles' feet, but he had preached that the money was used to preach the gospel in other cities. When he concluded, I lifted my head to heaven and asked, "Lord, where did he get that from?"

The question usually on the minds of most Christians who read this passage is, "If the early church gave to brethren why does the present day church not do the same?"

We have had instances of leaders in the world trying to create impressions to other countries while their countries burn within. They go speaking of peace and equality and justice in other nations, yet their nations rot from violence and injustice; they could lend to other countries just to create an impression, yet they have their streets littered with the homeless, the jobless, the beggars, the sick and they do not in one moment care whether they die or live. The same could be said of leaders in the church. They are all competing to make impression on the world outside the church while brethren suffer in silence. They boast of how rich the church has become; they invite you to check out their accounts, yet with them are brethren with no roof over their heads, no food to eat; youths in their midst are disillusioned because no one but God would help. Some churches carry out some hypocritical charity of going to look for the hungry, the naked, and the sick outside the church, while those in the house just pretend all is well. They have widows who cannot feed their kids, these are told to continue to sow and be more dedicated, the fatherless are told God would take care of them if they serve God dedicatedly. It is heartbreaking to mention the untold suffering brethren undergo in a house said to be full of meat. No one seems to care about the other Christian's well being because everyone is striving to give to

God to get more.

Pastors just care about having the number of members increased, they boast of the attendances to their ministry, they boast about the money they collect as tithe and offerings, but care less for the people from whom they collect them. They preach of the widow's mite, "she gave her all" they would say, so the brethren must give their all on the altar. "Laying all at the altar" is interpreted to mean giving all money and properties on the altar.

The lower currency denominations are rejected as offerings because, according to some preachers, God is too much for these small denominations. Jesus Christ tells the mind of God with the story of the widow who gave two mites:

And Jesus sat over against the treasury, and beheld how the people cast money into the treasury: and many that were rich cast in much. And there came a certain poor widow, and she threw in two mites, which make a farthing. And he called unto him his disciples, and smith unto them, Verily I say unto you, That this poor widow hath cast more in, than all they which have cast into the treasury: For all they did cast in of their abundance; but she of her want did cast in all that she had, even all her living. (Mark 12:41–44.)

Jesus Christ was not teaching us to give all, but sought to clear our judgmental attitude toward what people give. He sought to clarify that one who may have given the least in the eyes of man may have given the best in the sight of the Almighty. But in our churches, only the best givers are praised and commended. In fact, the only way to show commitment to God is now measure by how much money is given. That a Christians goes to church regularly and wins people for Jesus Christ does not count as much. This ought not to be!

A preacher sharing on giving told his audience that it is wrong to share out of the possessions brought to church to brethren in need. According to them, God got angry with him when he gave possessions given by brethren out to some members of the church. He recommended that all items given be sold and the money used for God's business only. Yet I have never known God as a shrewd father who would rather items brought to his house be sold instead of giving them to the church He gave his life to purchase. On the contrary, scriptures show that it is an abomination to sell what is brought to God's house. Items of the sanctuary were never sold; they could be eaten, but never sold.

Every page of the Bible tells about a God who is love, a God who cares for His people. If He can give His life, He can give anything. If the children of the house do not deserve to eat of the Father's meat, then who deserves to eat? Is it the businessmen that deal in exotic cars or some estate surveyors that have properties to sell or rent out, or some five star hotels that have beautiful conference halls, or the managers of stadiums in town or the television house where some preacher wants to be seen?

The first reason why brethren sold their possessions was to minister to brethren's needs. They were not sons of consolation only to Peter, or the other apostles, but to the people of God. The money was not given so that the apostles can go to neighboring cities to preach (at least God's Word did not say so) neither was it used to build another worship place because God brought in as many as should be saved, it was used to meet needs of the people that was added to the church.

The book of Acts tells what fellowship in the church was like in the beginning:
And all that believed were together, and had all things common; sold their possessions and goods, and parted them to

all men, as every man had need. And they, continuing daily with one accord in the temple, and breaking bread from house to house, did eat their meat with gladness and singleness of heart, praising God, and having favour with all the people. And the Lord added to the church daily such as should be saved. (Acts 2:44–47)

They had things in common; they sold their goods and possessions and parted them to all men as every man had need. They sold for the brethren. They gave primarily for the brethren, yet the Lord added daily to them such as should be saved. What brought souls to the church was not the city-wide crusades they organized; but as they dwelt together with one heart, having all things in common, the Lord added to them. I believe that if ministers would sometimes, use half of the money used for renting crusade venues to attend to brethren's need in church, they would have no need to orga-nize crusades. The news of a church that cares for the needy would spread like wild fire and what the church would worry about is the manifestation of the gift of the spirit to build the people that come in every day.

The reason for the appointment of deacons was to set someone over the daily ministration to the brethren.

And in those days, when the number of the disciples was multiplied, there arose a murmuring of the Grecians against the Hebrews, because their widows were neglected in the daily ministration. Then the twelve called the multitude of the disciples unto them, and said, "It is not reason that we should leave the Word of God, and serve tables. Wherefore, brethren, look ye out among you seven men of honest report, full of the Holy Ghost and wisdom, whom we may appoint over this business (Acts 6:1–3)

Stephen was appointed to manage the daily distri-bution of materials effectively, especially to the widows in the different places of worship. Peter would have called the ministration to the brethren "ministering to tables," yet he did agree that it was a business requiring urgent attention of not just mere men, but of those full of the Holy Ghost and wisdom. Yes, brethren may never be completely satisfied and will always murmur and complain, if ministering to brethren's need is not part of the vision from God to his shepherds, to what purpose is the appointment of deacons in our churches?

In his words of commendation to the church at Ephesus (Ephesians 1:15), Colossi (Colossians 1:4), Thessalonica (Thessalonians 1:3), and to Philemon, Paul spoke of the brethren's demonstration of faith toward God and love toward the saints: Brethren gave to one another. They had faith in God but gave to each other!

"We are bound to thank God always for you, brethren as it is meet, because that your faith growth exceedingly, and the charity of every one of you all toward each other aboundeth"
(2 Thessalonians 1:3)

MINISTERING TO THE APOSTLES

The early church also gave to meet the needs of the apostles. The brethren at Philippi of their own volition gave to Paul in the time of necessity.

"But I rejoiced in the Lord greatly, that now at the last your care of me hath flourished again; wherein ye were also careful, but ye lacked opportunity. Not that I speak in respect of want: for I have learned, in whatsoever state I am, therewith to be content. I know both how to be abased, and I know how to abound: every where and in all things I am instructed both to be full and to be hungry, both to abound and to suffer need. I can do all

things through Christ which strengtheneth me. Notwithstanding ye have well done, that ye did communicate with my affliction. Now ye Philippians know also, that in the beginning of the gospel, when I departed from Macedonia, no church communicated with me as concerning giving and receiving, but ye only. For even in Thessalonica ye sent once and again unto my necessity. Not because I desire a gift: but I desire fruits that mat abound to your account. (Philippians 4:10–17)

The brethren gave to Paul during his tribulation, not to tap into his anointing, but to bear with him in his time of need; Paul did not have to appeal or preach a sermon to have them give. Paul had learned to be content whether in want or in abundance. He was self sufficient in Christ. As far as he was concerned, it is part of ministry to suffer for Christ's sake. However, he commended the brethren for contributing to meet his needs and sharing with him his difficult times.

Ministering to Saints in other Churches

The early church gave for the welfare of saints within the same church and to churches in other towns and cities. The saints at Macedonia contributed materials, not to preach the gospel at Jerusalem, but to meet the needs of poor saints who lived there.

"For it hath pleased them of Macedonia and Achaia to make a certain contribution for the poor saints which are at Jerusalem" (Romans 15:26). They also minister to Paul's needs (2 Corinthians 11:9).

Paul "robbed" brethren in one gathering to do service to brethren in another gathering. The service Paul rendered may have been preaching the gospel to the brethren, he did not consider having to take from the brethren to preach the gospel a lawful thing to do, he considered it robbery; he called it "taking wages."

"I robbed other churches, taking wages of them, to do your service." (2 Corinthians 11:8)

For brethren in need in other gatherings, Paul could use strong words of appeal.

When Paul called on the Corinthians to give, it was toward the saints. "For as touching the ministering to the saints . . ." "Now concerning the collection for the saints . . ."

For as touching the ministering to the saints, it is superfluous for me to write to you: For I know the forwardness of your mind, for which I boast of you to them of Macedonia, that Achaia was ready a year ago; and your zeal hath provoked very many. Yet have I sent the brethren, lest our boasting of you should be in vain in this behalf; that, as I said, ye may be ready: Lest haply if they of Macedonia come with me, and find you unprepared, we (that we say not, ye) should be ashamed in this same confident boasting. Therefore, I thought it necessary to exhort the brethren, that they would go before unto you, and make up before hand your bounty, whereof ye had notice before, that the same might be ready, as a matter of bounty, and not as of covetousness. But this I say, He which soweth sparingly shall reap also sparingly; and he which soweth bountifully shall reap also bountifully, every man according as he purposeth in his heart so let him give; not grudgingly, or of necessity: for God loveth a cheerful giver. (2 Corinthians 9:1–7)

To the Corinthians Paul wrote, "Now concerning the collection for the saints, as I have given order to the churches of Galatia, even so do ye." (1 Corinthians 16:1)

Paul's emphasis on giving in these verses of scriptures was not toward God or his work but to the saints, the needy in God's house. This indicates that churches everywhere all over the world can care for one another, ministering to one another in material gifts so that no one lacks.

It is beautiful to learn that the popular Bible quotation on the mouth of every preacher, "He which soweth sparingly shall reap also sparingly; and he which soweth bountifully shall reap also bountifully." was in reference to saints in need not to a God in need.

The popular prayer, "Now he that ministered seed to the sower both minister bread for your food, and multiply your seed sown, and increase the fruits of your righteousness." was said with reference to those who would have dispersed abroad giving to the poor saints.

As it is written, He hath dispersed abroad; he hath given to the poor: his righteousness remaineth for ever. Now he that ministered seed to the sewer both minister bread for your food, and multiply your seed sown, and increase the fruits of your righteousness. Being enriched in every thing to all bountifulness, which caused through us thanksgiving to God. For the administration of this service not only supplieth the want of the saints, but is abundant also by many thanksgivings unto God; Whiles by the experiment of this ministration they glorify God for your professed subjection unto the gospel of Christ, and for your liberal distribution unto them, and unto all men; And by their prayer for you, which long after you for the exceeding grace of God in you. Thanks be unto God for his unspeakable gift.
(2 Corinthians 9:9–15)

Brethren in the church at Corinth gave to brethren in Macedonia supplying the wants of the saints with many thanksgivings onto God. Materials were given to saints while thanksgiving was onto God! It is the giving to the poor that is righteousness that remains forever (Psalm 112:9); giving to the saints is subjection and commitment to the gospel of Christ. Sowing on the grounds of the saints and of the needy is the evidence of God's grace in a man's life.

The early Church also gave toward every good work in the church (2 Corinthians 9:8) including church projects; but foremost in Paul's heart, were the brethren. When he spoke on giving in his letters to the churches, it was for the saints. Exhorting the Christians on what could be called the tenets of the Christian faith, "distribution to the necessity of saints" is deemed as vital as waiting on our ministry, arboring that which is evil, cleaving to that which is good, being kindly affectionate one to another, been fervent in the spirit serving the Lord and rejoicing in hope. It is as important as rejoicing in hope, patient in tribulation and continuing instant in prayer (Romans 12:7–14).

Chapter Seven

God blesses and increases the works of a man, who gives to a Christian in need. In Deuteronomy 15:7–11, He made bare His heart on the poor and needy in His house. His promise to Israel was to take them to a land flowing with milk and honey. But in spite of the prosperity of the land, God had said, "The poor shall not cease out of the land".

If there be among you a poor man of one of thy brethren within any of thy gates in thy land which the LORD thy God giveth thee, thou shalt not harden thine heart, nor shut thine hand from thy poor brother: But thou shalt open thine hand wide unto him, and shalt surely lend him Sufficient for his need, in that which he wanteth. Beware that there be not a thought in thy wicked heart, saying, The seventh year, the year of release, is at hand; and thine eye be evil against thy poor brother, and thou givest him nought; and he cry unto the LORD against thee, and it be sin unto thee. Thou shalt surely give him, and thine heart shall not be grieved when thou givest unto him: because that for this thing the LORD thy God shall bless thee in all thy works, and in all that thou puttest thine hand unto. For the poor shall never cease out of the land: therefore I command thee, saying, Thou shalt open thine hand wide unto thy brother, to thy poor, and to thy needy, in thy land. (Deuteronomy 15:7–11)

It is preached that God owes nobody yet he is a debtor to every one who gives to the poor. The needy are always in church in our midst. He who gives to the poor lends to his maker.

"He that hath pity upon the poor lendeth unto the LORD; and that which he hath given will he pay him again." (Proverbs 19:17)

There is giving and taking that tends to want. Taking from the needy amongst us instead of giving to them is not in line with the scripture.

"He that oppresseth the poor to increase his riches, and he that giveth to the rich, shall surely come to want." (Proverbs 22:16)

A church that oppresses the needy amongst them to increase the riches of the wealthy and fat would surely tend to want. What blessing is there in taking from brethren who cannot afford to pay their rent, send their kids to school, or put food on the table?

Jesus Christ taught on alms' giving to the needy:

Take heed that ye do not your alms before men, to be seen of them: otherwise ye have no reward of your Father which is in heaven. therefore when thou doest thine alms, do not sound a trumpet before thee, as the hypocrites do in the synagogues and in the streets, that they may have glory of men. Verily I say unto you, they have their reward. But when thou doest alms, let not thy left hand know what thy right hand doeth: That thine alms may be in secret: and thy Father which seeth in secret himself shall reward thee openly. And when thou prayest, thou shalt not be as the hypocrites are: for they love to pray standing in the synagogues and in the corners of the streets, that they may be seen of men. Verily I say unto you,
They have their reward (Matthew 6:1–5)

Sometimes, alms in form of clothes, food, and money collected in the name of the weak and needy never get to them. If carefully observed, most of the used items like clothes, shoes exported or imported into country are donations to the weak and needy in various countries. Whoever or whatever organization had collected them sold them for money. The same applies in some of the churches today; help offering which is supposedly taken to help the needy in church is ploughed back into the church treasury. The materials never get to the needy unless they are not good enough to be kept or sold.

I worshiped in a church where the preacher gave a word of knowledge instructing that the church give toward the education of some brethren requiring financial assistance. The congregation responded to the call. However, the needy did not get to hear how much was given, let alone tasted what was given. We counted the money as part of the offering for the day and paid it to the bank next day. Paying school fees for the brethren was never mentioned after that. The church collected help materials monthly, but the church would rather give the materials to people outside the church. Most of the Brethren who went to the Helps Department in time of need were turned down. In fact, I do not remember anyone getting help at all because what ever was collected as help offering may have been used to settle other church expenses.

I thought the collection of help offerings for the poor outside the church a show-off thing. It was just another style of evangelism. We wanted to show people outside that we cared, but those who responded to the show of love and joined the church left eventually because; the love did not exist for those inside the house.

GIVING TO PASTORS

God has ordained that those who preach the gospel live by the gospel! We are supposed to take care of our leaders especially those who lay down their lives for the gospel.

In the ordinance of tithes and offerings, God ordained that those who attend to the altar should live by the altar and made adequate provision for them. In spite of the humility and sacrifices of Paul, when responding to some brethren who examined him, he emphasized that no one goes to war at his own charges; he pointed out that whoever plants a vineyard should eat of the fruit thereof and he who feeds the flock ought to eat of their milk. He supported his argument with the law "Thou shall not muzzle the mouth of the ox that treads out the corn" (1 Corinthians 9:9).

"Do ye not know that they, which minister about holy things, live of the things of the temple? And they, which wait at the altar, are partakers with the altar?" (1 Corinthians 9:13)

Pastors are God's servants called to tend his flocks. They minister to the church's spiritual needs and should reap of the church carnal things. That is the way God has ordained it! However, in spite of the authenticity of his argument, Paul wrote:

But I have used none of these things: neither have I written these things, that it should be so done unto me: for it were better for me to die, than that any man should make my glorying void . . . What is my reward then? Verily that, when I preach the gospel, I may make the gospel of Christ without charge, that I abuse not the power in the gospel . . . But I keep under my body and bring it into subjection: lest that by any means, when I have preached to others, I myself should be a cast away. (1 Corinthians 9:15, 18 and 27)

Paul knew he was entitled to receiving gifts from the brethren, yet he would ask no one to minister to his need because, according to him, doing so will make void his glory in Christ. To Paul, taking or asking from the brethren was taking a charge for preaching the gospel to them. He feared that preaching the gospel of Christ with a charge to it would make him a cast away before Jesus Christ.

It is possible to let Paul's words pass without understanding the import of his statement. Pastors and everyone who is called to lead must take this to heart. It is possible to raise the dead, heal the sick, win the whole world for Jesus Christ, and yet be a cast away if one ties a charge to doing it! If you think everyone ought to give to you because you are doing God's work, then you would have earned your reward here on earth and there would be nothing to glory in when you stand before the Father. A pastor who has become so rich by taking from the people would have earned his reward already.

When Paul agued the rights of the minister to the things of the altar, he based his points on the traditions of the Old Testament altar. But in Hebrews 13:10, he showed us that any man that is called to minister with Jesus Christ on the New Testament altar has no right to eat anything of the altar. The New Testament altar demands the sacrifice of them that minister therein. They must be willing to take up the cross, follow Jesus Christ, and lay down their lives as He did.

In his last speech to the brethren at Ephesus in the book of Acts, Paul said,

I have coveted no man's silver, or gold, or apparel. Yea, ye yourselves know, that these hands have ministered unto my necessities, and to them that were with me. I have shewed you all things, how that so laboring, ye ought to support the weak, and to remember the word of the Lord Jesus Christ, how he said, 'It is more blessed to give than to receive. (Acts 20:33–34)

Paul's admonition was not to everybody in the church,

for verse seventeen says he called for the elders, admonishing them to take care of all the flock over which the Holy Ghost had made them overseers, to feed the church of God which he had purchased with His own blood. He reminded the elders of the words of the Lord Jesus Christ that it is more blessed to give than to receive.

Take note of Paul's words! Though an apostle, his hands labored to earn income not just for himself but also for the flocks that were with him. In his laboring for the gospel, he supported the weak and needy; he remembered that Jesus Christ had taught that it is more blessed to give than to receive. Paul did not boast of giving to God's work only, he also supported the brethren.

Giving in God's house is so designed that the shepherds do not neglect the wants of the sheep; and the sheep, that of the shepherd. All giving whether to the weak and needy, or the pastors must be given freely and cheerfully.

Like the saints in Philippi ministered to Paul's need, it is important to minister to the needs of our pastors. It is a responsibility. Just as God would not tolerate a pastor neglecting his sheep, he would also not smile at the church neglecting His pastors. There ought to be a balance.

But where a church continues to buy cars after cars, build houses after houses, give gifts after gifts to pastors while brethren wallow in poverty, God will not hold the shepherds of that church guiltless.

God lamented in Ezekiel 34:2, pastors who would rather feed themselves than the church.

"Thus saith the Lord GOD unto the shepherds; Woe be to the shepherds of Israel that do feed themselves! Should not the shepherds feed the flocks?"

What is the rationale behind a pastor or leaders of a

church, making budget to purchase the latest car in town for thousands of dollars? A machine that is here today and is not tomorrow has no eternal value. In contrast, the same money could be used to turn the destiny of many people around and leave them eternally grateful to God.

Pastors should learn from a leader like David who could not drink the water of Bethlehem even though he had longed for it because two men had risked their lives to get him the water. Pastors do not have to accept every gift from God's people because only God is worthy of them. God said of the princes of Israel in Isaiah 1:23, "Thy princes are rebellious, and companions of thieves." What made them companions of thieves? God said of them "Everyone loveth gifts and followeth after rewards, they judge not the fatherless, neither doth the cause of the widow come unto them."

There is nothing like sowing into a pastor's anointing or gifts of the spirit. There is no record of anyone doing it in the scriptures. The anointing comes with the Holy Ghost and with knowledge of the things that are freely given unto us as Christians.

A pastor who takes gifts sowed unto him would have to answer to the Holy Ghost who is the anointing because he trades the Lord's Holy Spirit for gifts. Paul said, "Lest that by any means, when I have preached to others, I myself should be a cast away" This popular scripture is in reference of taking from the church. Pastors are going to be surprised when they stand before the Lord thinking to get a reward only to be told that there are no such records, as they would have received their rewards already.

The fact that the anointing was not in the power of the carrier to transfer at will was demonstrated when Elisha requested a double portion of Elijah's anointing. The beneficiary of the anointing is determined by the anointing Himself.

"And he said, Thou hast asked a hard thing: nevertheless, if thou see me when I am taken from thee, it shall be so unto thee; but if not, it shall not be so." (2 Kings 2:10)

There is nothing as sowing into the anointing, but there is sowing unto the saints. The former is unscriptural and by analogy, worldly!

If the church has adopted the tradition of tithe and offering, then it must fulfill it to the fullest. Those who bring tithes are supposed to eat them (their tithe) in God's House. If they adopt the tradition of giving as the early church did, the brethren come first in the administration of things given. Whether we teach on giving in the Old or New Testament way, the flocks of God take preeminence.

"For whosoever shall keep the whole law, and yet offend in one point, he is guilty of all" (James 2:10)

Leaders call for offering to build church buildings, pay for centers for programmes, put on advert, and hold programmes on TV all over the world. They build resting places for men who are renowned, but without a single plan to cater for God's people in need. This is sycophancy; it is the same as what happens out there in the world amongst world leaders. The brethren are made to build houses they would never be allowed to enter even in times of need. They buy cars they would never ride in except they pay a fare.

God's Words to David and Solomon showed what very little respect God may have for the buildings we prefer to build rather than care for the needy in the church. God never asked to be built a house. The Bible said David thought of building God a house after that the Lord had given him rest round about from all his enemies (2 Samuel 7:1). God said to David through the prophet Nathan,

. . . Shall thou build me an house for me to dwell in? Whereas I have not dwelt in any house since the time that I brought up the children of Israel out of Egypt, even to this day, but have walked in tents and tabernacles. In all the place wherein I have walked with the children of Israel spake I a word with any of the tribes of Israel, whom I commanded to feed my people Israel, saying, why build ye not me an house of cedar?" (2 Samuel 7:5–7)

With these words, God showed He had little use for a house. However, He showed what His heart desire was: to give David a name and give His people Israel a home!

Moreover I will appoint a place for my people Israel, and will plant them, that they may dwell in the place of their own, and move no more; neither shall the children of wickedness afflict them any more, as before time. (2 *Samuel 7:10*)

However, He accepted the idea of having a house in His name; He promised David that his seed after him would build the temple. When God visited Solomon the night after the dedication of the temple, the first thing He swore to destroy was the very building built if Solomon would not walk in his statutes (2 Chronicles 7:20–22). According to the desires of his father David, Solomon had set out to build the Lord's house and several other palaces for himself and his queen at the same time. Building the temple took seven years (1 Kings 6:38). His personal palace took thirteen years (I Kings 7:1) including his other house at Lebanon and the palace for his queen (1 Kings 7:8). For this course, he levied the people of God.

And King Solomon raised a levy out of all Israel; and the levy was thirty thousand men. And he sent them to Lebanon, ten thousand a month by courses: a month they were in Lebanon, and two months at home: and Adoniram was over the levy. And Solomon had threescore and ten thousand that bare burdens, and fourscore thousand hewers in the mountains; Beside the chief of Solomon's officers which were over the work, three thousand and three hundred, which ruled over the people that wrought in the work (1 Kings 5:13–16)

There was a levy on the people of Israel to bring in great stones, costly stones, and hewed stones to build the temple. For twenty years of Solomon's forty years reign in Israel, (1 Kings 9:10) the people lived under this burden. It must have been so heavy that they begged Jeroboam, Solomon's son for relief.

It is good to build churches for God. However, of greater importance to Him is shepherding His people and bringing them to a place of rest. I believe that God would have no glory in the building of towers in His name at the expense of His people because He does not dwell in buildings made by hands but in the very hearts of the people we tend to neglect.

Brethren who are rich and fat have become so eager to give to God in order to receive multiplied harvest that they have become blind toward their needy brethren. A church could raise millions to pay to hold a day's programme but would frown at raising a thousand to give a roof over a member's head. They are zealous to give to a television programme, or another church abroad, but frown at buying a plate of food for the brother who is hungry. Some say the weak and needy in the church are lazy and so would not help them in time of need! Brethren see large sums of money stashed away every day, yet they hunger, and their brethren would do nothing.

The church would breed thieves because they would be tempted to steal even from the "sacred offerings" to survive. Recently, I heard of thieves breaking into churches during and after church services and brethren have lost their lives defending the sacred offering from been taken away by the invaders. They cart away instruments bought at some astronomical amounts of money. All it takes is have a pastor announce the cost of the equipment and the next day, the equipment disappears.

Why is it so easy to give out money to a God whom we do not see but find it so difficult to help brethren in need? "If a man says, I love God, and hateth his brother, he is a liar: for he that loveth not his brother whom he hath seen, how can he love God whom he hath not seen?" (1 John 4:20)

Is love to the brethren just in the saying "I love you" in our fellowship meetings or is it just about visiting them to encourage them to attend the next meeting? John in his letter to the church expounded on what love toward the saints should be.

But whosoever hath this world good, and seeth his brother have need, and shutteth up his bowels of compassion from him, how dwelleth the love of God in him? (1 John 3:1–17)

Loving God is not just preaching His Word throughout the earth; it is laying down our lives for the brethren. Loving the brethren is not just singing, dancing, and sharing the Word of God together; it is not shutting up our bowels of compassion from them in time of need. It is sharing with them our possessions. A church that can boast of spending large sum of money for programmes but have flocks living hopelessly in lack has no business talking about love.

How can the church continue to lock up her bowel of compassion from the weak and needy in her mist and still preach the gospel of the Lord Jesus Christ? The pastors, instead of ministering to the widow, the fatherless, the needy, preach them into borrowing to sow seeds for their prosperity.

It has never been a blessing to borrow. A Christian is subject to the one from whom he or she borrows. He that is blessed of the Lord lends.

James, talking to Christians who would rather preach and pray for their needy while they stash away millions in banks and live in great affluence said,

What doth it profit, my brethren, though a man say he hath faith, and have not works? can faith save him? If a brother or sister be naked, and destitute of daily food, And one of you say unto them, Depart in peace, be ye be warmed and filled; notwithstanding ye give them not those things which are needful to the body; what doth it profit? Even so faith, if it hath not works, is dead, being alone.
(James 2:14–17)

Here is what James is saying: you are a preacher, you perform all the works of faith, you can preach with signs following and yet you do not tend to the physical needs of the people you minister to, then that faith is dead.

The phrase "Faith without works" does not apply only to the faith required to receive a miracle as it is taught in most churches. James reference to "faith without works" was in respect of love toward the brethren. You may have healed or won thousands of souls, when taking care of them physically is not part of the plan, that faith is dead. As a church, do you have millions in bank accounts and yet keep praying to God to bless and feed the needy among you? This is sheer hypocrisy. To call for the little they have to live on when you have millions stashed away in some account is spiritual cruelty! It is faith without works! It is dead faith.

In Isaiah 2:14–15, God said He would enter judgment with the ancient of His people and with the princes thereof because they have eaten up the vineyard and have the spoil of the poor in their houses. He did not condone taking the goods of the poor in the time past; He would not condone it now.

PLEDGES AND FREE WILL OFFERINGS

The priest, the Levites, and the people ate tithes and offerings according to the Law. For the building and maintenance of the tabernacle, the people gave willingly, everyone as they had determined in their hearts. Moses called on Israel to give, as they will toward the building of the tabernacle.

And they came, every one whose heart stirred him up, and every one whom his spirit made willing, and they brought the LORD'S offering to the work of the tabernacle of the congregation, and for all his service, and for the holy garments. And they came, both men and women, as many as were willing hearted, and brought bracelets, and earrings, and rings, and tablets, all jewels of gold: and every man that offered an offering of gold unto the Lord. And every man, with whom was found blue, and purple, and scarlet, and fine linen, and goats' hair, and red skins of rams, and badgers' skins, brought them. Every one that did offer an offering of silver and brass brought the Lord's offering: and every man, with whom was found shittim wood for any work of the service, brought it. And all the women that were wise hearted did spin with their hands, and brought that which they had spun, both of blue, and of purple, and of scarlet, and of fine linen. And all the women whose heart stirred them up in wisdom spun goats' hair. And the rulers brought onyx stones, and stones to be set, for the ephod, and for the breastplate; The children of Israel brought a willing offering unto the LORD, every man and woman, whose heart made them willing to bring for all manner of work, which the LORD had commanded to be made by the hand of Moses. (Exodus 35:21–29)

Beside the feast of the Sabbath and tabernacles, other thing the children of Israel could bring to the Lord included, gifts, freewill offering and vows (Leviticus 23:37–38). Scriptures reveal that the Sabbath, the feast of tabernacle, the bringing in of gifts, and freewill offering will be an everlasting practice of the sons of God; and if we consider these three, they are gestures which emanate from the individual toward a beloved. They are not forced, or commanded. They are just expression of love toward God. So should be every giving by the Christian.

In the same manner, Paul exhorted that in giving, every man should give, as he will determine in his heart. Pledges and free will offerings can be made for projects in the church. Even Gentiles gave to building of the walls, gates, and sanctuary in the Bible. These pledges were not only in the form of money, they came in the form of manual contributions to the work at hand. The church is the family of God and it is every Christian's responsibility to give to every good work in the house of God including the financing for places of worship, organizing outreaches etc. Yet, God's minister should be considerate in laying out the plans for giving.

For instance, a pastor who requests pledges toward a building today, and calls for pledges for a crusade next week, and another request to finance a wedding some other week and another request to give toward a love feast in the same week would in no doubt produce people who give murmuring.

I have been to a church where they collect tithe and offering in every kind of meeting. After the collection some brethren come, demanding moneys for an item forcefully sold to brethren during the meeting. Then there is a request to contribute toward paying for a generating set rented earlier for the service; another follows with collection for pastor's refreshment or for transportation fare to a programme after church meeting; some others could follow with another collection for stationery for the church office. Everyday brethren had to give to some kind of project.

The pastor of this church would not fund any project from the church purse even tough brethren gave so much because he wanted to be able to give so much to the headquarters to obtain praise and promotion. Not before long, brethren started leaving the church, those who stayed murmured against him.

Like the government of a nation plans its budget, the church should plan their budget and spread it out, putting the people into consideration. This is not faithlessness.

Gifts Sharing in the Church

The Bible gives us an idea of God's position on things in His house when He gave instructions to Moses on the sharing of the spoil from the war with the Midanite.

And the LORD spake unto Moses, saying, Take the sum of the prey that was taken, both of man and of beast, thou, and Eleazar the priest, and the chief fathers of the congregation: And divide the prey into two parts; between them that took the war upon them, who went out to battle, and between all the congregation: And levy a tribute unto the LORD of the men of war which went out to battle: one soul of five hundred, both of the persons, and of the beeves, and of the asses, and of the sheep: Take it of their half, and give it unto Eleazar the priest, for an heave offering of the LORD. And of the children of Israel's half, thou shalt take one portion of fifty, of the persons, of the beeves, of the asses, and of the flocks, of all manner of beasts, and give them unto the Levites, which keep the charge of the tabernacle of the LORD. And Moses and Eleazar the priest did as the LORD commanded Moses.
(Numbers 31:25–36)

Half of the gift went to those who fought or worked to bring in the bounty. The second half went to the people. A heave of what was shared to the men of war and the people went to the Levites and the priests. Everyone in God's house benefited from gifts to the house of God. I sincerely believe that He has not changed His mind. If He is the selfish God preachers project Him to be, He would have instructed that everything be dedicated to His house, but as uncountable as Israel was, the gift in the house was shared to great and small, everyone partook of the bounty. Church leaders must learn and decide to appropriate the things in God's house to everything and everyone. That is the way God wants it done. It is funny to watch a lot of gifts waste away in churches because the minister could not decide what to do with them. Due to the teaching on how sacred such gifts are, some ministers find it easier to send gifts brought to church to the overseer in the ministry than share it amongst God's people. Where the gift is not good enough for the overseer, it is allowed to waste in the church store. This is painful to know in a house where one look into the eyes of people reveals pains and hopelessness from hunger and lack. The gifts brought to God's house should be portioned out to all of God's people who might have needs for them. This is scriptural.

Chapter Eight

In Matthew 6:20, Jesus Christ said, " . . . But lay up for yourselves treasures in heaven, where neither moth nor rust doth corrupt and where thieves do not break through and steal."

Laying treasures in heaven is a phrase in the mouth of every preacher when they speak on giving in the church. Jesus Christ showed us how to lay treasures in heaven in the encounter with the rich man.

And when he was gone forth into the way, there came one running, and kneeled to him, and asked him, Good Master, what shall I do that I may inherit eternal life? And Jesus Christ said unto him, Why callest thou me good? there is none good but one, that is, God. Thou knowest the commandments, Do not commit adultery, Do not kill, Do not steal, Do not bear false witness, Defraud not, Honour thy father and mother. And he answered and said unto him, Master, all these have I observed from my youth. Then Jesus Christ beholding him loved him, and said unto him, One thing thou lackest: go thy way, sell whatsoever thou hast, and give to the poor, and thou shalt have treasure in heaven: and come, take up the cross, and follow me. (Mark 10:17–21)

Jesus Christ invited the rich to sell all he had and give the proceeds to the poor. By so doing, he would have treasures in heaven. It is popularly preached that whatever is given to God's work is laid up as treasures in heaven. If this were true, then Jesus Christ would have invited the man to sell all he had and put into God's work that He Jesus Christ, was doing. He required funds to preach the gospel from city to city, and would have been grateful if the rich man gave to Him. Instead, He told the rich man to sell all he had and give to the poor. Only then would he have treasures in heaven.

And in Luke 12:33, he said to the multitude that listened to Him preach,

Sell that ye have, and give alms; provide yourselves bags which wax not old, a treasure in the heavens that faileth not, where no thief approacheth, neither moth corrupteth. For where your treasure is, there will your heart be also.

Jesus Christ shows the way to lay up treasures in heaven–It is not by preaching or winning souls, it is by giving our all to the poor, the weak, and needy in the church. The Bible says those who win souls shall shine like the stars forever, but those who give to the poor lay up treasures in heaven.

Jesus Christ buttressed the way to build up treasures in heaven by the parable of the sheep and the goats.

THE SHEEP AND THE GOAT

Jesus Christ spoke of the last days when He will come to judge the world. The basis of judgment would not be who sinned and who did not. We would be surprised to know that judgment would be based how much love and mercy and kindness we showed to His brethren.

When the Son of man shall come in his glory, and all the holy angels with him, then shall he sit upon the throne of his glory. And before him shall be gathered all nations: and he

shall separate them one from another, as a shepherd divideth his sheep from the goats: And he shall set the sheep on his right hand, but the goats on the left.

Then shall the King say unto them on his right hand, Come, ye blessed of my Father, inherit the kingdom prepared for you from the foundation of the world: For I was an hungered, and ye gave me meat: I was thirsty, and ye gave me drink: I was a stranger, and ye took me in: Naked, and ye clothed me: I was sick, and ye visited me: I was in prison, and ye came unto me. Then shall the righteous answer him, saying, Lord, when saw we thee an hungered, and fed thee? or thirsty, and gave thee drink? When saw we thee a stranger, and took thee in? or naked, and clothed thee? Or when saw we thee sick, or in prison, and came unto thee? And the King shall answer and say unto them, Verily I say unto you, Inasmuch as ye have done it unto one of the least of these my brethren, ye have done it unto me. Then shall he say also unto them on the left hand, Depart from me, ye cursed, into everlasting fire, prepared for the devil and his angels: For I was an hungered, and ye gave me no meat: I was thirsty, and ye gave me no drink: I was a stranger, and ye took me not in: naked, and ye clothed me not: sick, and in prison, and ye visited me not. Then shall they also answer him, saying, Lord, when saw we thee an hungered, or athirst, or a stranger, or naked, or sick, or in prison, and did not minister unto thee? Then shall he answer them, saying, Verily I say unto you, Inasmuch as ye did it not to one of the least of these, ye did it not to me. And these shall go away into everlasting punishment: but the righteous into life eternal. (Matthew 25:31–46)

It is amazing to note that the goats do not refer to people who do not believe in Christ, but they are believers who ignore the hungry, the thirsty, the stranger, the naked, and the sick in the church. Look at it! Jesus Christ did not say when I was hungry you taught me God's Word on how to prosper and never be hungry, instead he said "I was hungry and ye gave me meat" Jesus Christ did not say I was sick and you prayed for me or taught me to receive divine healing. He said, "I was sick, and ye visited me."

Though there is a regard for every good work, Matthew 25:34 did not say that the Kingdom of God is not prepared for pastors, apostles, evangelists or prophets, or faith healers or those who sow seeds; but for those who feed the hungry, visit the sick, take in the stranger, cloth the naked and visits those in prison. Verse forty-one of the same chapter tells what happens to a church or ministry who ignores the hungry, the naked, the sick, and the stranger in the church.

Teaching the needy in our midst to give to pave way to their prosperity could be a dangerous path to tread. The church cannot be tired of taking care of them because Jesus Christ actually points it out as one thing that touches His heart. One way to pave our way into the kingdom of God is through giving to His people.

Reading through Matthew 7:21–23, it is surprising to note that prophesying or working miracles is not evidence of doing God's will, but giving to His people, in every way is. Oh, I thank God daily for giving the church His pastors. Life would have been unbearable without miracles wrought in the name of Jesus Christ by His shepherds. Seeing the tears of joy twinkle down the faces of brethren because of the miracle of healing, deliverance, and supply makes serving Jesus Christ sweeter and blissful. Yet, Jesus Christ said:

Not everyone that saith unto me, Lord, Lord, shall enter into the kingdom of heaven; but he that doeth the will of my Father which is in heaven. Many will say to me in that day, Lord, Lord, have we not prophesied in thy name? and in thy name have cast out devils? And in thy name done many wonderful works? And then will I profess unto them, I never knew you: depart from me, ye that work iniquity"

But the kingdom of God is prepared for those who concern themselves with caring for the household of faith. Jesus Christ did it, Peter did it, Paul did it, and every shepherd will have to follow in this track.

Matthew 24: 45–51 tells the reason why the Lord would set a servant over his household. One reason may have been to keep the house in order, but the Bible did not say so; it did say that the reason is to give them meat in due season. The servant does contrary to his lord's instruction if he begins to smite his fellow servants, and to eat and drink with the drunken.

FINDING THE BALANCE

Jesus Christ showed a balanced way to living a godly life. He likened paying tithe and offering of mint and rue and neglecting justice and mercy to cleaning the outside of a cup and leaving the inside dirty. The inside is made clean by giving to the needy in our mist; then, is the whole church truly clean.

And the Lord said unto him, now do ye Pharisees make clean the outside of the cup and the platter; but your inward part is full of ravening and wickedness. Ye fools, did not he that made that which is without make that which is within also? But rather give alms of such things as ye have; and, behold, all things are clean unto you. But woe unto you, Pharisees! for ye tithe mint and rue and all manner of herbs, and pass over judgment and the love of God: these ought ye to have done, and not to leave the other undone. (Luke 11:39–42)

The Pharisees were leaders of God's people, yet Jesus Christ rebuked them for striving to live rightly by paying tithes and offerings while neglecting mercy toward the poor.

I once heard it preached that tithe should be given of gifts and presents received. Yet giving to the needy amongst God's people is a burden too much for the church to bear. Jesus Christ teaches that a church is not complete just taking tithe of its members; it must also minister mercy and justices toward the church. Mercy is being touched with their feelings of infirmity; justice is letting them have their place in God's house and giving to them, that which pertains to them.

The Bible also gave a definition of what makes pure and complete Christianity:

"Pure religion and undefiled before God and the Father is this, to visit the fatherless and widows in their affliction, and to keep himself unspotted from the world." (James 1:27)

A church that believes in tithing and giving to God, owes God's the duty of making the meat available to God's people. This is complete and whole religion.

Galatians 6:10 admonish that as much as lies in our power, we must do good especially to the household of faith.

If God's shepherds would sincerely look through the Bible with an honest heart, they would find out that God expects so much from them toward his sheep. When Jesus Christ rose from the dead and appeared to Peter by the sea, He said, "Feed my sheep" (John 21:15–17). God's primary reason for calling for every form of giving is to provide meat in His house, not only for the Aarons and programmes in His church, but more importantly, for the people He gave his life to purchase including the needy, the widow, the fatherless, and the stranger in His house.

THE MAN HEAVEN COVETS

The book of Acts accounts of a Gentile - a Roman Centurion - who feared God and served Him through prayers and giving of much alms to the people.

There was a certain man in Caesarea called Cornelius, a centurion of the band called the Italian band, A devout man, and one that feared God with all his house, which gave much alms to the people, and prayed to God alway. He saw in a vision evidently about the ninth hour of the day an angel of God coming in to him, and saying unto him, Cornelius. And when he looked on him, he was afraid, and said, What is it, Lord? And he said unto him, Thy prayers and thine alms are come up for a memorial before God. (Acts 10:1- 4)

Cornelius feared God, he prayed and loved the people. Heaven could not just let him alone; he was someone special God wanted to identify with. God sent Cornelius an angel and Peter to bring him into His fold. His prayer and alms came before God as a memorial. Heaven could not wait to make Cornelius heir of salvation. The Holy Ghost came upon him and his household as Peter preached salvation in Jesus Christ.

Daniel in the wisdom of the spirit showed us a secret and the power behind caring for and giving to God's people:

Wherefore, O king, let my counsel be acceptable unto thee, and break off thy sins by righteousness, and thine iniquities by shewing mercy to the poor; if it may be a lengthening of thy tranquility (Daniel 4:27)

When the King Nebuchadnezzar was revealed the evil that was intended against him in a dream interpreted by Daniel the prophet, he was shown a way of escape from the evil that was by the "decree of the watchers and the demand by the word of the holy ones" (Daniel 4:17). One way of escape was to show mercy to the poor.

Peter confirmed this in 1 Peter 4:8 when he said, "And above all things have fervent charity among yourselves: for charity shall cover the multitude of sins."

The giving to the poor as a way of breaking iniquities is usually criticized; yet, it is scriptural and God approved of this in Isaiah, chapter fifty-eight.

A Better Way to Fast and be heard

So important to God is the caring for the needy in our homes, in our environment, in our churches that one can attribute the sufferings in the most nations of the world, our homes and churches to our neglect of the weak, the home-less, the widow, the children, and the strangers in our midst.

The way to fast is not by hiding from our bodies, or from our flesh, or from our loved ones; it is not by afflicting our souls and abstaining from food. A church could go on fasting for a hundred days and may have their prayers unan-swered. God gave a secret way to fast and receive answers to prayers: The way is to give our bread to the hungry, bring the poor that are cast out to our houses, clothe the naked and not hide ourselves from our flesh, draw our soul to the hungry and satisfy the afflicted soul.

Then will our countries, churches, homes break forth as the morning; our health shall spring forth speedily, our righteousness shall go before us and the glory of the Lord shall be our reward.

Then we will call and the Lord will answer if we will

remove the yoke and the harsh speaking from the Church. Our light will rise in obscurity and our darkness will be as the noonday. The Lord will guide us continually and satisfy our soul in drought and make fat our bones (Isaiah 58:1–11).

Blessings will come upon our homes, our country, our jobs and businesses if we will just look in the way of the weak and needy. The command to give the poor and needy brings with it showers of blessings including wealth, health and prosperity.

THE GIVING THAT RAISES THE DEAD

There was a disciple in Joppa called Tabitha interpreted Dorcas (Act 9:36- 41). The Bible records that this woman was full of good work and alms deeds.

Note that Dorcas was not said to be holding crusades, we were not told she was going for door to door evangelism or gave so much money to help the apostle preach from place to place; the Bible said she did charitable works in God's House - ministering to the weak and needy in the church.

Dorcas became sick and died. The brethren washed her and kept her in the upper room; they could not bury the love that had cared for them. They could not just let death take away one person who cared for them. The brethren, learning that Peter was in Lydda, sent for him begging him to come and not delay.

When Peter came to the brethren, all the widows stood by him weeping and showing the coats and garment, which Dorcas made for them. Peter did not need a special anointing, he prayed and presented her alive to the widows. Good works toward the saints of God raised Dorcas from the dead.

The power of the Spirit will be so immense in the Church if church leaders with all sincerity and integrity of hearts cater for God's people. How can you keep billions in your account and each day you keep praying to God to feed the needy in your church? What makes you think that He listens or hears those kinds of prayers? If we preach that God has given the church the authority to rule on earth: to preach, heal and raise the dead, why would it be God's duty to help the weak and needy in church? If we cannot stand by the needy in church, whom then do we expect to help them?

Times when we have managed to talk on giving to the brethren, it is as though God is talking to the people as individual Christian and not as a church. But the Holy Spirit has shown us through the early church that His Church could actually come together as a people to face the material challenges in the lives of believers. We can do it! If the early church gave and no one lacked in a church of more than three thousand souls, then the present day Church can do much better. If we can raise millions in one church service to hold a programme in some hotel, what stops us from raising the same millions to help people in church? I think the time has come when the church should sit down and plan. The plan must include meeting every material need of the flock. My observation is that the Church does not take caring for God's flock as part of ministry. That is why even when we know that people are going through so much trouble and their faith is being tried, we just stand by, watch, and expect God to either come down from heaven or perhaps send the heathen as answers to the needs of brethren. We just watch some simple material needs make God's Word a lie in the life of the brethren.

It amuses me how preachers preach and jump past any verse that refers to giving back to God's people. They would preach on the people honoring their leaders and ignore the fact that Jesus Christ had taught that anyone called to lead or minister is supposed to be a servant of the brethren. The

whole essence of ministry is the people. Yet, the people are often considered not important. Otherwise why would we build one house after the other, buy one car after the other, make one trip after the other, finance one programme after the other, while the people have no shelter, no food to eat, and no clothes to wear. The pastors would fight to sustain what they call their ministry and vision while running rough shod over the people in the ministry, collect whatever they can to sustain that vision even if it takes bringing God's people under poverty.

God in the history of nations never tolerated the oppression of the weak, and needy: for the neglect of the fatherless and widow and the orphans in nations, God would rise to defend them from those that puff at them (Psalm 12:5). Neither will He tolerate it in His church - His body. He said in Isaiah 1:11–17,

To what purpose is the multitude of your sacrifices unto me? I am full of burnt offerings . . . Incense is an abomination . . . the new moon and the Sabbath, the calling of assemblies . . . it is iniquity, even the solemn meeting . . . When you make many prayers, I will not hear . . . Put away the evil of your doing before my eyes, cease to do evil, learn to do well, seek justices, relieve the oppressed, judge the fatherless, plead for the widow.

All our sacrifices and offerings, all our church activities and prayers will be of no use to God when the needy, the fatherless and the widow are deliberately neglected in the church or in any nation at that. The conventions and the crusades may become disenchanting unto God if the church would not learn to do well. The ruler of nations of the earth and shepherds of God's church must take decisive steps toward taking care of people over whom God has made them overseers. The blessing and prosperity of every nation, church, and home lie in nothing else but in justices

and mercy toward these groups of people.

If taking tithes of God's people is one way the church must make meat available in God's house so let it be! But the tradition must be executed fully and the order in the sanctuary of God followed to the letter. The overseers, Presidents, Founders of churches have a portion. Then the Levites - all Pastors and church workers also have their portion. The people - the tithe payers, widows, the fatherless, and the strangers - must partake of the meat in God's house.

"Aaron," you are not entitled to all but to a tenth of the tithe of the tenth to the Levites. It is wrong to watch your church workers live by faith while the tithes are signed away to car dealers, television stations owners, estate surveyors, rentals, hotel managers who perhaps earn a lot of their profits from churches. The meat in the house is not for your vision only; but for God's vision, which is His church. No matter what we think, the church comes first in God's mind. True, He wants people out there to be saved. The crusades and adverts on television stations would bring them; but only true and sincere love would keep them in the church. Jesus Christ said, "By this shall all men know that ye are my disciples, if ye have love one to another" (John 13:35).

Workers in the ministry are entitled to a tenth of the tithes, offering, and gifts that comes to the house of God. It is their portion as long as the church keeps collecting tithes and offerings.

God's people, the beloved of the Lord, are entitled to most part of the tithes, gifts and offerings. However, this it is not a license for Christian to sit and do nothing! Christianity is responsibility. Bible says God is able to make all grace abound to you, so that in all things and at all times having all that you need you will abound unto every good work. Just as we strive as Christians to have a good name before God, we should put the most of our efforts into making sure we never have to beg or become a burden to the church.

Pledges should be made for building and major works in God's House. Giving to these projects is everybody's responsibility. Yet, for anyone who thinks building a big worship place at the expense of caring for God's flock a big deal, learn from King Solomon! Of great importance to God was Solomon walking before Him and shepherding His people Israel in integrity and uprightness of heart, otherwise the building did not mean a thing.

It is so easy to want to acquire more properties in the name of Jesus Christ; buy more land, build more offices or places of worship, and buy the most expensive cars because God is not a poor God. Yet, the shepherds of God can also plan to feed the hungry, clothe the naked, and shelter the homeless in the House of God. Churches can build highly subsidized schools, medical centers, and places of shelter for God's people. The dreams for the ministry should extend to projects that better the lives of God's people. Part of the purse or treasury could be reserved to help God's people in time of need. It should not be too much burden to give toward the betterment of God's people. They are people we profess to love every time we preach. Love is not in word, but in deeds.

It is indeed true that the church required "mega bucks" to preach God's Word to all the nations of the earth and the "mega bucks" will have to come from God's people as God prospers them. Pastors can raise the "mega bucks" required to do God's work without bringing back the law of the spirit of death into Christianity and hinging God's promises on what is given. Like the Holy Ghost teaches through Paul, everyone should give, as they shall determine in their hearts. Of course, he that sows sparingly shall reap sparingly and he that sows bountifully shall reap bountifully. For as the heaven and the earth remains, seed and harvest time shall never cease. But the wrath that the law works in the heart of the men of God toward his flock must cease and the church made free from the law of the devourer. The devourer will devour, not because God has willed it so in this dispensation of grace, but because the shepherds over God flocks have determined that they will not let go. We should remember that when God appeared to Elijah after the three and half years of drought. God's message to Elijah was, " . . . Go, shew thyself to Ahab; and I will send rain upon the earth." (1 Kings 18:1). But the calling of fire from heaven to devour and the killing of the prophets of Baal was Elijah's own plan. That fire came from heaven to destroy as commanded by Elijah does not make it God's plan.

The Church will have to find a balance between expanding God's kingdom and shepherding the souls in the kingdom. It is not enough to just win souls for Jesus Christ, there is need to shepherd them according to God's plan and make the dwelling place of God a home for His sheep.

GOD BLESS HIS CHURCH. AMEN!

Contact author Akadin Prudence
or order more copies of this book at

&

TATE PUBLISHING, LLC

127 East Trade Center Terrace
Mustang, Oklahoma 73064

(888) 361 - 9473

Tate Publishing, LLC

www.tatepublishing.com